The Natural History of

WILD SHRUBS
and
VINES

Other books by Donald W. Stokes

A Guide to Nature in Winter
A Guide to the Behavior of Common Birds

The Natural History of
WILD SHRUBS
and
VINES

Eastern and Central North America

DONALD W. STOKES

Illustrations by Deborah Prince Smith

1817

HARPER & ROW, PUBLISHERS, New York

Cambridge, Hagerstown, Philadelphia, San Francisco,
London, Mexico City, São Paulo, Sydney

THE NATURAL HISTORY OF WILD SHRUBS AND VINES. Copyright © 1981 by Donald W. Stokes. Illustrations © 1981 by Deborah Prince Smith. All rights reserved. Printed in the United States of America. No part of this book may be used or reproduced in any manner whatsoever without written permission except in the case of brief quotations embodied in critical articles and reviews. For information address Harper & Row, Publishers, Inc., 10 East 53rd Street, New York, N.Y. 10022. Published simultaneously in Canada by Fitzhenry & Whiteside Limited, Toronto.

FIRST EDITION

Designed by Sheila Lynch

Library of Congress Cataloging in Publication Data

Stokes, Donald W.
   The natural history of wild shrubs and vines.
1. Shrubs—United States. 2. Climbing plants—
United States. 3. Plant lore—United States. I. Title.
QK482.S84   582.1'70973   80-8219
ISBN 0-06-014163-8

81 82 83 84 85 10 9 8 7 6 5 4 3 2 1

CONTENTS

CONTENTS

PREFACE

DURING MY TRAINING to become a naturalist I started my study of plants by becoming familiar with trees and then continuing on with wildflowers. Over the years I began to feel knowledgeable about most of the major plants in these two categories. I was about to take on the more specialized groups, such as the ferns and mushrooms, when I suddenly realized that there was a large and abundant group of plants that I was totally ignoring. It was the shrubs and vines. I had passed them by in favor of the more majestic trees and the more delicate wildflowers. For some reason, I thought that shrubs and vines were both uninteresting and hard to identify. After realizing that this was just a prejudice, a prejudice shared by most of my fellow naturalists, I became determined to find out about the lives of these plants. What were they really like?

With the aid of a marvelous book by George W. D. Symonds, *The Shrub Identification Book* (William Morrow & Co, New York), I found that shrubs and vines were really quite easy to distinguish, especially in certain seasons. And there were far fewer that were common than I had thought. After learning the names of the more common varieties, I wanted to know all about their natural history. What habitats do they like? What plants do they live near? What mammals or birds use them? How have humans used them? How do their seeds disperse? How did they get their common names?

I spent many months searching for a book that would answer these questions, and came to the surprising discovery that there was none. It was then that I decided to write it myself.

The book concentrates on shrubs and vines that grow naturally in the wild. These plants are described at the genus level rather than at the species level for two reasons. First, because there is very little known of the natural

PREFACE

history of many species and, further, because plants in the same genus often share much of their natural history.

Although there are many helpful clues to identification in the text and illustrations, this book is not designed to be a guide to identification in the field. For this, the Symonds book does an excellent job, and I saw no need to duplicate that work. Rather, this book is most helpful after you know the name of a plant and can go out and examine it as it changes through the seasons. You can start with the familiar plants you may already know, such as Rose, Blueberry, Grape, and Sumac. Read the sections on these plants and I am sure that the text and illustrations will make you want to go back out and look more closely for the interesting features of their natural history. Then, as you learn the names of other plants, include them in your explorations, and use the book to help in your discovery of their lives. I have included descriptions of the shrubs and vines in all seasons, and I encourage you to visit your favorite plants throughout the year to get a more complete picture of their interactions with other living things.

Through writing and researching this book I have become more aware of the wealth of enjoyment that these plants offer even the casual observer. Now, instead of being an undifferentiated mass of vegetation that I look past to find trees or wildflowers, the wild shrubs and vines have become an exciting group of individuals that I look forward to seeing and examining on each of my walks through the woods. I hope this will happen for you, too.

DONALD W. STOKES

Carlisle, Massachusetts, 1980

The Natural History of

WILD SHRUBS
and
VINES

JUNIPER

Juniperus

ORDER: *Coniferae.*   FAMILY: *Pinaceae.*   GENUS: *Juniperus.*
SPECIES: *J. communis,* Common Juniper.

POPULAR NAMERS really missed an opportunity to give Common Juniper some pithy name, for it is one of the most ornery plants in old meadows, its needles being sharp, its stems low to the ground and hard to cut. Maybe something like "Field's End" would have been appropriate, suggesting that once Juniper has moved in, there is little hope of easily clearing the land. But the only names we have are Common Juniper and Ground Juniper, and these are far too bland for such a distinctive plant.

Common Juniper is most frequently found in old rocky meadows and on mountainsides, above the treeline. It is a low evergreen shrub whose branches spread horizontally and, where they touch the ground, often send down roots. In open areas, the plant forms dense, barely penetrable thickets. These serve as cover for small mammals and valuable roosting and nesting sites for birds. If you ever have to walk across one of these thickets you will find it difficult, for Juniper branches are tough and springy and not quite dense enough to create good footholds. The experience is similar to that of walking on the exposed springs of an old mattress.

Common Juniper is one of the few shrubs in eastern North America that has evergreen needles. In winter, you will notice that the needles most exposed to the sun turn a lovely rust brown, while those more in shade remain green. In the summer, all return to being green. Why this color change occurs is still not well understood. You will also notice that each needle has a bright white line on one of its surfaces. These white lines are actually made up of hundreds of openings (stomata) that control the flow of water and gases in and out of the needle. The needles are arranged in

§ 1 §

Common Juniper growing among rocks

whorls of three, with successive whorls rotated 60 degrees from each other, so that when you look down the stem you see the needles forming a six-pointed star.

Common Juniper flowers are almost impossible to detect at any more than a few feet from the plant. In fact, you may be looking right at them and not realize that they are flowers. The flowers are unisexual—that is, male and female are borne on separate plants. The male flowers are tiny globular buds no more than a quarter of an inch across. They are similar to catkins and have no petals or scent, since their pollen is carried on the wind. One of the best ways to detect the flowers is to knock the boughs of the plant on a dry day in May or June and to look for pollen drifting into the air. Sometimes I find solitary bees buzzing around male Junipers, feeding on the pollen. The female flowers are harder to recognize, for they are even smaller and produce no pollen.

§ 2 §

JUNIPER

Once pollinated, a female flower develops into a small cone with fleshy scales. All fruits on members of the Pine family—Pine, Spruce, Hemlock —start as a cluster of fleshy scales. With most species, the scales eventually dry out and the fruit comes to look like the typical woody cone. In the case of Juniper, however, the scales remain fleshy and the fruit looks more like a berry, even though it is structurally a cone.

When the fruits ripen in late summer, they are about a quarter inch in diameter and blue, covered with a white, powdery bloom. In the winter months, you might even mistake them for a dusting of snow upon the spreading branches. The dried cones of the other members of the Pine family disperse their seeds in the wind, but Juniperus, by keeping its fleshy scales, attracts animals, which eat its fruits and pass on the seeds in their droppings. If you watch birds feeding on the fruits, you will discover that different species eat them in different ways. Robins, Jays, and Mockingbirds just pick off the fruits, tilt their heads back, and swallow them whole. Chickadees, on the other hand, hold the fruits in their feet, peck out the seeds, and let the fleshy pulp fall to the ground. Mice and Red Squirrels also eat Juniper fruits, and the Red Squirrel is reported to depulp the seeds just as the Chickadee does.

Fruits and needles of Common Juniper

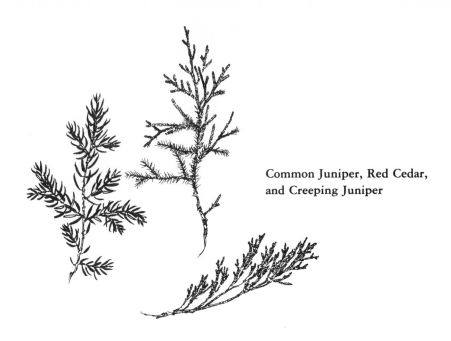

Common Juniper, Red Cedar,
and Creeping Juniper

You are likely to find some fruits that have grown especially large. Pick one of these and take a careful look at it. You may find the fruit has a small hole; when you open it, you will see that it is hollow and filled with tiny black particles. Some of the other large fruits will have no holes in them, and inside, a small larva will be eating away. All this is evidence of a small wasp called a Chalcid Fly, a species that lays its eggs in the developing Juniper fruits. The larva feeds and grows inside the fruit, then bores a hole to the outside and leaves. The black particles in these fruits are the larva's droppings. The distorted fruits that have housed the wasp larvae are considered galls and called Juniper Berry Wasp Galls.

For hundreds of years, Juniper fruits have been used for seasoning in stews and with meats. They are also traditionally the main flavoring of gin and can be used to make a Juniper "berry" tea. Before you leave the plant, take the opportunity to pick one of the fruits and crush it between your fingers. They have a rich, resinous smell, one reminiscent of Christmas and holiday greens—a nice association to carry with you as you continue on your walk.

GREENBRIER

Smilax

ORDER: *Liliiflorae.*   FAMILY: *Liliaceae.*   GENUS: *Smilax.*
SPECIES: *S. Walteri,* Red-berried Greenbrier;
S. rotundifolia, Horsebrier; *S. Bona-nox,* Bullbrier;
S. tamnoides, China-Root; *S. glauca,* Sawbrier;
S. laurifolia, Laurel-leaved Greenbrier.

YOU MIGHT THINK it just a bad joke if someone told you Greenbrier was good to eat, for through most of the year it is a woody vine with tough tendrils and sharp thorns. But every spring, I make a point of going out to gather a few of Greenbrier's growing tips, one of my favorite woodland snacks. At that stage, the thorns, stems, tendrils, and leaves are all tender, with the clean, crisp taste of fresh greens. By early summer the growing tips are tough and woody and no longer palatable to us, but this does not keep deer from continuing to browse the plant, one of their favorite foods. Sometimes Greenbrier is so heavily browsed that it appears as little more than short green stalks with thorns.

Greenbrier is easy to identify in all seasons: it is the only woody vine in the East with both thorns and tendrils. It grows in areas between woodlands and an open space, such as roadsides, forest edges, and riverbanks. Like most vines, it uses other woody plants for support, rather than developing thick stems of its own. Pairs of tendrils growing from the base of each leaf attach to the branches of trees and shrubs, helping the vine to hold on as it climbs up into the sunlight.

Recently I have become fascinated by the forms of twisting in tendrils. I was led to this interest by reading a chapter in *Eye Spy* by William Hamilton Gibson. Writing in 1897, Gibson pointed out that most people assume tendrils just coil like springs; the method is, in fact, far more interesting and complex. Each tendril has two stages of movement. First,

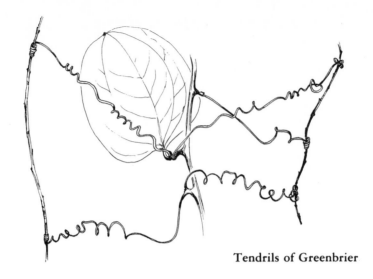

Tendrils of Greenbrier

the tip forms a tight coil around a support. The middle of the tendril then starts to twist, but since both ends are fixed, it cannot coil like a spring. To understand what the tendril is forced to do, take a piece of rope, attach one end to an immovable object and hold the other. With your free hand, twist the middle of the rope. Two spirals will soon form, one on either side of where you are twisting. The spirals will go in opposite directions, and where they meet at your fingers will be a short straight section. This is the form of coiling that occurs in Greenbrier tendrils. Attached tendrils develop two or more adjacent spirals twisting in alternate directions; between spirals, there are straight, untwisted portions. Tendrils that have finished twisting become incredibly tough, while those that never coil around supports usually wither and hang off the vine like delicate threads. The next time you are near Greenbrier, take a moment to do some tendril-watching. You can extend this activity to Grape, as well, since its tendrils twist in the same way.

Greenbrier's flowers—small, light green, and almost odorless—are easy to miss. Look for them in early summer; they grow from the leaf axils and are arranged in spherical clusters at the end of short stalks. A close examination will reveal that the flowers are unisexual, the sexes borne on separate plants. Pollination is carried out by small insects, especially flies.

§ 6 §

GREENBRIER

In fall, you will notice mature fruits on the vine—small, hard berries arranged in spherical clusters, just like the flowers. They are dark blue or black in all species except the Red-berried Greenbrier. As you open the fruit, you will find small seeds, each enclosed in an elastic membrane. If you squeeze the seed in the membrane and slowly pull your fingers apart, rubbery filaments will form. This phenomenon has led people in some areas to call the plant Stretchberry. Cleaned of pulp, the seeds are hard and shiny; in the past, they were used by the American Indians as beads for necklaces. The fruits remain on the vine through most of the winter and are only occasionally eaten by birds.

Greenbrier leaves, when they first emerge, are shiny and light brown, looking as if they have been dipped in shellac. Many species retain this gloss through the summer, and the light reflecting off these leaf surfaces make areas of Greenbrier particularly beautiful on sunny days. Popular guidebooks distinguish the six woody species of Greenbrier by reference to the leaves—their shapes and the different colors of their upper and lower surfaces. But this method is not always helpful, since leaf shapes vary within

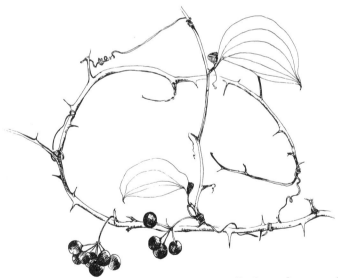

Fruits and stems of Horsebrier

species and leaf colors are impossible to compare when you have found only one plant. There are few easy ways to distinguish the species, so if you have trouble with it don't be discouraged; it is not a reflection on your abilities but rather on the similarities within the genus.

Laurel-leaved Greenbrier is the only evergreen member of the genus in North America. All others shed their leaves in fall. The Greenbriers are unusual among our woody plants in the way that their leaves are shed. With most other trees and shrubs, the whole leaf stalk (petiole) breaks away from the twig, and the resulting scar is sealed with a corky layer to preserve moisture. In Greenbriers, the base of the leaf stalk remains attached to the vine, while the center of the stalk withers and the leaf eventually breaks off at that point. It is interesting to speculate whether this process is a more primitive form of leaf shedding or one that is transitional between the evergreen and deciduous habits. Young deciduous Oaks often shed in both ways, some leaves breaking off at the twig and others breaking off at the middle of the petiole.

Another feature of Greenbrier in fall is the ripened tubers or swellings that occur on the roots. The great naturalist John Bartram (1699–1777) reported being given a drink by certain southern American Indians that was made from ground Greenbrier tubers. He said that the Indians also made fritters from a mixture of the ground tubers and corn meal. The largest tubers are found on southern species such as Laurel-leaved Greenbrier or Bullbrier. They are best collected in the fall of their first year; soon after, they become tough and unpalatable. They are believed to function as food storage areas that may help the plant survive the winter or aid in producing new shoots the following spring.

Although Greenbrier may persist even when it is overshadowed by a developing forest, its best growth occurs where there is plenty of sunlight. Sometimes it even forms impenetrable walls of thorny green stems at forest edges. Although this may be an inconvenience to you when you're out walking, it is an asset to birds, providing a protected site for their nests. So before you detour around one of these tangles of vines or leave Greenbrier after observing its natural history, take a moment to peer in among the leaves for nests, especially the large stick nests of Brown Thrashers and Catbirds, species that are particularly fond of Greenbrier thickets.

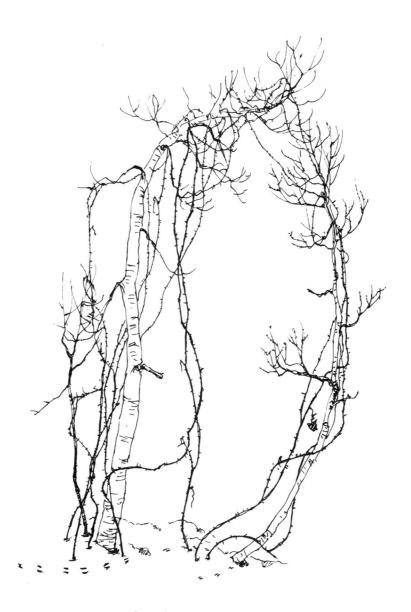

Greenbrier in winter

WILLOW

Salix

ORDER: *Salicales.*   FAMILY: *Salicaceae.*   GENUS: *Salix.*
SPECIES: *S. lucida,* Shining Willow; *S. interior,* Sandbar Willow;
S. discolor, Pussy Willow; *S. sericea,* Silky Willow;
S. candida, Hoary Willow; *S. purpurea,* Basket Willow,
and many others.

IF IN LATE WINTER you become tired of the cold, sunless days and the dulled colors of the landscape, bundle up with an extra scarf and head out to where Willows grow. You will find them lining roadside ditches or bordering open ponds and sunlit streams. Not only are their clusters of fine yellow or red-brown stems a colorful sight, but their buds, with soft silvery hairs poking out of them, are also a sure sign of the coming spring. These furry growths are actually dense groups of minute petalless flowers, called catkins. In a few weeks, some will develop a covering of bright orange or yellow pollen. These are the male flowers. The female flowers are borne on separate plants. When mature, they are a soft light green.

Willow flowers are adapted to insect pollination and must therefore advertise their presence. To attract insects, the male catkins make themselves conspicuous by remaining vertical on the branch and having a covering of brightly colored pollen. Also, both sexes of catkins secrete nectar, ensuring that some insects will move between male and female plants and carry out pollination. The most common pollinators of Willows are bees in the family *Andrenidae.* These insects emerge early in spring and are often called solitary bees, for they live singly, rather than in large colonies like Honeybees.

A number of other catkin-bearing plants—such as Hazelnut, Bayberry, Sweet Fern, and Alder—are adapted to wind pollination. The male catkins

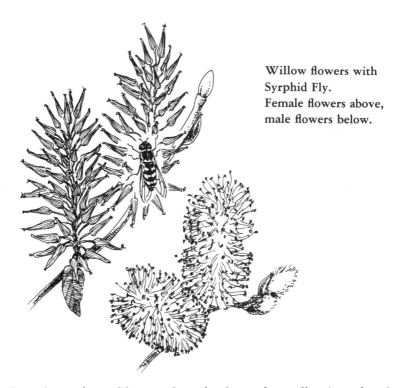

Willow flowers with
Syrphid Fly.
Female flowers above,
male flowers below.

of these plants hang down like tassels and release dry pollen into the air; their female catkins are usually small, erect, and shaped like miniature pine cones. With no particular need to be conspicuous, these flowers do not secrete nectar or have bright colors.

By late spring, the Willow's female catkins have already matured hundreds of minute seeds. The seeds are surrounded with white, cottony fibers that help to keep them airborne when they are dispersed by the wind. Look for the airborne seeds in May or June, resembling bits of cotton floating in the summer breeze. May and June are also when Yellow Warblers build their nests of downy plant materials, and if you are fortunate, you may see one traveling back and forth between female Willows and its nest site, its beak full of the cottony fibers each time it leaves the Willow.

The Willow genus contains both trees and shrubs, the difference in classification being primarily one of size and the number of trunks. Trees are large, usually with a single trunk, while shrubs are smaller and often have many trunks growing from the same spot. A characteristic unique to

§ 11 §

Yellow Warbler gathering
Willow fluff for its nest.

all Willows, one that will help you identify them in practically all seasons, is that their leaf buds are covered with a single scale, rather than many scales, as is the case with most other plants. These buds, which contain the leaves and flowers for the following year, start to grow in midsummer and remain on the plant until they open the following spring.

There are more than fifty species of Willows in the East, and since many of them hybridize, identifying a particular plant can be extremely difficult. The character of the leaves is the feature most often used to distinguish species. Willow leaves may emerge before, during, or after the blooming of the flowers. In general, they are long, thin, and pointed at the tip; at their bases there are often pairs of small leafy appendages called stipules. Because the traits of the leaves and stipules alone may not be sufficient for a final identification, a detailed examination of the flowers and/or mature seeds may also be necessary. In any case, you surely do not need to know the species name before you start to enjoy the natural history of the genus.

Only a few weeks after Willow leaves emerge, you are likely to find them riddled with holes or distorted in some way: for some unknown reason, Willows are particularly attractive to insects. One of the earliest eaters of the leaves is the larva of the Mourning Cloak. This butterfly overwinters as an adult, emerges early in spring, and lays its eggs on Willow shrubs. The larvae soon hatch and feed communally, aligned side by side and

WILLOW

perpendicular to the leaf edge. Another insect found on the leaves in early summer is a small, iridescent-blue, leaf-eating beetle, called the Shining Willow Beetle, *Plagiodera versicolora.* It is an imported beetle that is now widespread, and while it is found most often on Willow trees, it is also present on some of the shrub species. All four of its life stages can be detected on the leaves, from yellow eggs, to black larva, to pupa, to shining adult.

Willows have always been useful plants for humans. For example, Willow suckers grow rapidly, sometimes as much as four feet in a single season.

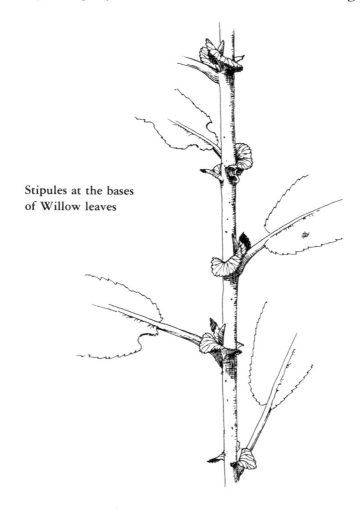

Stipules at the bases
of Willow leaves

These new stems are strong and flexible and have been used widely for making baskets. One European species was imported to this country because of its particularly supple twigs; its common name is Basket Willow. The roots of Willows, fibrous and wide-spreading, grow even faster than the stems. They are excellent at holding soil and so are often planted to control erosion in wetlands. People have found a medicinal use for Willows as well. For hundreds of years, a substance has been extracted from the bark and used as a pain reliever. In the 1800s, the bark was discovered to contain salicylic acid, the chemical from which aspirin was eventually derived.

In fall and winter, when Willows have shed their leaves, you will notice some unusual growths at the tips of the twigs. These are galls—deformations of plant tissue caused by the physical actions or chemical secretions of insects. The Beaked Willow Gall, an almond-shaped swelling about an inch long with a tuft or beak at its tip, is caused by a gall gnat, *Phytophaga rigidae.* In early summer, the fly lays its eggs singly on the tips of Willows. After hatching from an egg, the larva burrows into the twig, stimulating the plant to produce the gall. The larva then hollows out a chamber in the gall, and makes a passageway through the beaklike projection. It finally seals off the passageway with silk and crawls back into the chamber, where it spends the winter. In spring, it pupates in the gall, and after transforming into an adult fly, leaves through the tunnel in the beak. If you see small or otherwise abnormal Beaked Willow Galls, it is likely that the gall-maker has itself been parasitized, which has stopped or altered the normal formation of the gall.

The Petaled Willow Gall and the Pine Cone Willow Gall are also formed by gall gnats, *Rhabdophaga brassicoides* and *R. strobiloides* respectively. They are two of the most beautiful galls to be found in winter. The Petaled Willow Gall looks like a woody flower and the Pine Cone Willow Gall like a miniature smooth-scaled pine cone. Both are formed on the terminal buds of twigs and the life histories of both the gall-makers are similar: in spring, the adult fly lays an egg on the tip of an actively growing twig; the hatched larva burrows into the plant and by chemical or physical irritation causes the gall to form; the larva overwinters in the gall, pupates in early spring, and emerges as an adult.

One of my favorite discoveries on Willows is the winter home of the

From left to right:
Pine Cone Willow Gall,
Petaled Willow Gall,
and Beaked Willow Gall

Viceroy Butterfly. Look along the bare branches of the Willow shrubs. If you see any small bit of leaf attached to the twigs and if the petiole of the leaf is actually tied to the twig with silk, then you have found the butterfly's winter quarters. In fall, the young caterpillar took a leaf, reinforced its connection to the twig, and ate away the tip of the leaf on either side of the midrib. It then folded the base of the leaf into a tube and crawled in for the winter. The caterpillar is only about a half inch long at this stage. In spring, it will become active and complete its life cycle by feeding on new leaves, pupating, and then emerging as an adult. The adults lay their eggs only on members of the Willow family (which includes Poplars).

As well as being a summer food for insects, Willows are an important winter food for birds and mammals, especially those that live in the far

WILLOW

north. In these areas, Willows are often the dominant plant, and are tall enough to stick up through the snow, thus providing winter buds for Grouse to eat, and twigs and bark for Snowshoe Hare, Beaver, White-tailed Deer, and Moose to browse. In summer, these same Willows form dense cover, which is valuable for the protection of nesting wildfowl that have migrated north for their breeding season.

Willows, clearly, are marvelous plants, but they are also more than just the sum of their natural history. The common phrase "bend like a willow" comes from our observation that Willows withstand the force of floods and storms by bending and being supple. Willows have come to represent, in a more general way, the use of flexibility rather than rigidity to deal with external forces, an idea that might well be applied to our own lives.

Adult Viceroy Butterfly
and winter hibernacula

BAYBERRY, SWEET GALE

Myrica

ORDER: *Myricales.*   FAMILY: *Myricaceae.*   GENUS: *Myrica.*
SPECIES: *M. gale,* Sweet Gale; *M. pensylvanica,* Bayberry;
M. heterophylla, Evergreen Bayberry; *M. cerifera,* Wax Myrtle.

THE GENUS *Myrica* contains two very different groups of plants: the Bayberries, which typically have wax-coated fruits and live by the sea or along inland lakes; and Sweet Gale, which has small nutlets for fruits and grows in the shallows of swamps and bogs. One of the most pleasant things about this genus is that all its members have fragrant resin glands on their leaves, fruits, catkins, or stems. In any season, there is always some good smell that one can get from rubbing a part of these plants—the leaves in summer and the fruits, catkins, or buds in winter. I never pass by a member of this genus without touching it and taking advantage of this gift that the plants offer.

Bayberries are, of course, best known for their berries. The waxy coating of the fruits is actually a type of fat containing large amounts of palmitic acid, a substance also found in palm oil and in spermaceti, the oil found in the head of the Sperm Whale. In colonial times, this was boiled off the fruits and used to make bayberry candles. Real bayberry candles are a beautiful light beige, and when they are burned, their fragrance is subtle and sweet, not heavy or overpowering as with so many commercial candles. Our bayberry candles today are no longer made from native plants, for their berries yield too little wax to make them profitable to harvest; the ingredients come from other species in South America and Europe, which have a higher proportion of wax.

Bayberry fruits are eaten by a great variety of birds in fall because the

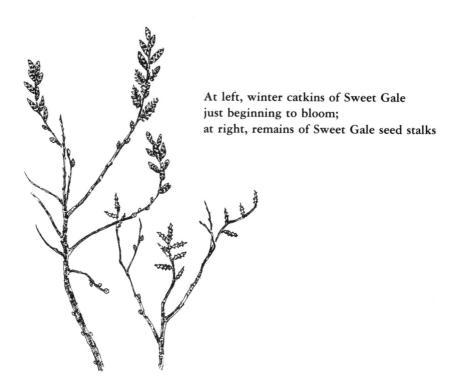

At left, winter catkins of Sweet Gale
just beginning to bloom;
at right, remains of Sweet Gale seed stalks

Atlantic coast, where the plants are common, is a popular migration route to the south. However, the only bird species known to make the berries a substantial part of its diet is the Tree Swallow, a bird that feeds primarily on aerial insects throughout the summer. It is interesting that the swallow has such a radical change in its food habits in fall. Possibly something in the fat content of the berries supplies the birds with important energy for their migration.

The three common species of Bayberry in the East all live in sterile, sandy soils, either along the coast or along the shores of inland lakes such as the Great Lakes. The Bayberry, *M. pensylvanica,* is the most northern among them, ranging from North Carolina to Newfoundland and Nova Scotia. The other species, Evergreen Bayberry, *M. heterophylla,* and Wax Myrtle, *M. cerifera,* grow from New Jersey south to the Gulf Coast.

Sweet Gale is more widespread than the Bayberries, growing throughout the northern half of North America, as well as in northeastern Asia and northwestern Europe. It is particular about its habitat, growing almost

BAYBERRY, SWEET GALE

exclusively in wet acid conditions, such as in the still water of lakes, swamps, or bogs, or in places where there is moist, peaty soil. In these areas, it usually spreads by extending rootstocks that send up new shoots. Over the years, this type of vegetative reproduction creates large islands of the plants out in the open water.

While Bayberries and Sweet Gale generally have unisexual flowers borne on separate plants, Sweet Gale is particularly interesting in that some individual Sweet Gale plants show an amazing amount of variation in this pattern. The catkins of Sweet Gale are borne on short terminal stalks, and although the majority of plants have either all male or all female flowers, some have both stalks with male flowers and stalks with female flowers. Others have male and female flowers on the same stalk. Still other plants may have flowers with both male and female organs in the same flower, but with only one sex functional. Finally, some of the plants actually have bisexual flowers. This one species of plant, therefore, displays the entire

Bayberries in late fall

Fruits of Sweet Gale
in late summer

range of sex separation in plants. Added to all this variation is the fact that
some plants of Sweet Gale that have had exclusively female flowers in the
past have been observed to change in subsequent years to having primarily
male flowers.

Sweet Gale, and to some extent the Bayberries, have nodules on their
roots, which (in conjunction with bacteria) are able to fix nitrogen from the
atmosphere and convert it to a form useful to plants. It is believed by some
scientists that given the wide distribution of Sweet Gale across the north
and the plant's ability to fix nitrogen, it may have played an important part
in enriching the soil of glaciated areas.

One of my favorite times to visit Sweet Gale is in winter, for at this time
its male catkins are particularly beautiful. Their scales are a dark ebony, and
each is edged with a light gray which highlights the tight spiral pattern they
form to enclose the flowers within. And of course, there is their fragrance.
If you rub the catkins gently with your bare fingers and then smell your
fingertips, you will get a whiff of the marvelous spicy odor common to the
whole genus. This is especially striking in the winter, when most of the
smells from nature are stilled by the cold air.

SWEET FERN

Comptonia

ORDER: *Myricales.*   FAMILY: *Myricaceae.*   GENUS: *Comptonia.*
SPECIES: *C. peregrina,* Sweet Fern.

SWEET FERN is not actually a fern but a flowering shrub, found typically in dry, sunny places where the soil is poor or has been recently disturbed. Look for it in the corners of old fields, along electric-line right-of-ways, and on the exposed banks created where roads are cut through the landscape. Its common name derives from the resemblance of its leaves to the leaflets of various ferns. In many ways, Sweet Fern is a pioneer plant. It colonizes areas that have been stripped of vegetation, where it helps enrich the soil, for its roots, like those of its close relatives, Bayberry and Sweet Gale, have the ability to join with bacteria in transforming atmospheric nitrogen into a usable form, thereby making it readily available to other plants. Sweet Fern also helps hold the soil together, since it spreads by a system of underground roots that continue to send up new shoots. This shoot system accounts for the fact that you will usually see small groves of the plant rather than just individuals. Other plants that thrive in the same habitat as Sweet Fern include Gray Birch, Low-bush Blueberry, Huckleberry, and Bracken Fern.

Be sure to visit Sweet Fern in winter, for its summer leaves often remain on the plant and create a striking design. Usually, they are dried into curls on the upper stems and interspersed with other shoots spiraled with winter catkins. From a distance, their lovely deep red-brown color is a pleasant contrast to the snow and the dried winter grasses. Return in earliest spring and you will find that the plant, now in bloom, has taken on a soft, furry quality. The expanded male catkins droop down, releasing pollen on the drier days. The female flowers, which are farther back on the same twigs, resemble tiny pine cones. They point upward, collecting pollen that is blown by on the wind. After blooming is completed, the new spring leaves emerge from their buds.

Sweet Fern's fruits always take me by surprise, for clustered together they look exactly like the gall that grows at the tips of Meadowsweet, *Spiraea.* Each seed is enclosed in a papery casing that has a number of points projecting from it. If you look among the leaves in midsummer, you can find this seed head. It is green then but turns brown by fall and may remain on the plant through the winter.

Of all the smells in the woods, my favorite is that of the leaves of Sweet Fern. The best time to get their full fragrance is in spring or fall during the early morning hours when dew covers the leaves and the sun is just beginning to strike them. Once, on just such a morning, I knelt down, held my head above the plants, and inhaled. Instantly I was carried away to special places of my past as only a scent remembrance can do. Another way to enjoy the scent of Sweet Fern is to lie downwind of the plants on a hot

Fruits and catkins of
Sweet Fern in winter

Fruits of Sweet Fern in summer

summer day and to let an occasional breeze carry the scent of the sunbaked leaves over your face.

For more than a year, I was mystified whenever I examined the leaves of Sweet Fern. In both summer and winter, I kept finding bunches of leaves held together with webbing. Inside this mass were insect droppings and a small, tough case shaped like an urn. The case was made from webbing and the feces of the insect. I regularly checked new groves of Sweet Fern to see if this phenomenon was widespread or just local. It seemed to occur in many vastly different areas, but always on Sweet Fern. When I opened these cases in winter, I always found a small orange larva, but in midsummer all I found in them was an empty brown pupal case. The mystery was solved one day when I was reading S. W. Frost's book *Insect Life and Insect Natural History* (1959). Frost describes a whole genus of small moths that tie leaves together and live through winter in a case made of webbing and covered with their own droppings. The genus is called *Acrobasis;* one of its species, *A. comptoniella,* incorporates the Latin name of Sweet Fern in its specific name. The moth lays its eggs on the plant in summer, the larva ties leaves together as it feeds on them, then makes a case in which it overwinters.

One warm spring day I decided to try making Sweet Fern tea. I had read that you could collect the leaves and steep them in water in the sun. I went to an area where I thought the plant might grow and soon found a small

§ 23 §

patch. I was reluctant to collect leaves there since it might have weakened the small stand, but nearby, at a much larger clone, I began to gather a few leaves from each plant. The next day, I put them in a mason jar filled with cold water, covered the top, and let the mixture brew for four hours in the morning sun. I shared the tea with friends during lunch. It was light green in color and, as is the case with many wild teas, the fragrance was stronger than the taste, but it was a pleasant, mild drink, slightly warmed from the sun.

While drinking the tea, I thought about the experience of collecting and preparing wild foods. The taste of the beverage was agreeable, but it was surely not something I would have bought in a store. Still, there was so much more to this experience than the taste alone. First there had been the search, which had involved knowing something about the habit of the plant; then there had been the picking of the leaves, the harvest, and the care taken not to hurt the plant I was enjoying; there was also the recipe, the formula recording what humans had learned to do with this plant over the centuries; and there was using the sun, thinking about the sun so that the jar would be warmed continually for four hours; and at last there was the result and the tasting. This process was so much more than the product. It was a way of experiencing more simply and deeply our connection with life around us.

Summer nest of *Acrobasis comptoniella* among the leaf tips of Sweet Fern

HAZELNUT

Corylus

ORDER: *Fagales.*   FAMILY: *Corylaceae.*   GENUS: *Corylus.*
SPECIES: *C. americana,* American Hazelnut;
C. cornuta, Beaked Hazelnut.

THERE IS A JEWEL of bright crimson in the late winter woods that should not be missed. It appears around the time when Spring Peepers start their choruses from swampy areas, when Willows and Aspens expand their catkins. It is the female flower of the Hazelnut, easily overlooked at a time when few think to search for blooms on plants. You are more likely to see the male flowers first, for they are long, drooping catkins that turn a soft yellow-brown as they mature. Brush them with your hand on a dry day and their pollen will drift into the air. Some male catkins hang down as much as four inches, while others are only an inch or so long. Once you have noticed them in bloom, then begin your search for the female flowers.

If you look closely at buds along the ends of branches, one will soon catch your eye, for projecting from its tip will be numerous bright red pistils. Though the flower is no more than a quarter of an inch across, I consider it one of our most beautiful. Its color is unmatched, except possibly by the blooms of the Red Maple, which start to open just a few weeks later. The female flower has no petals, but a cluster of small stigmas projecting in all directions. This lack of petals can be explained by the fact that the flower is wind pollinated and so does not have to attract insects, but it need only catch out of the air the pollen grains released from the male catkins. Not only are Hazelnut flowers among the earliest to open, they also last longer than most, remaining in bloom long into spring. Seeking them out may become as much a ritual for you as it is for me, especially if you live in the north, where spring seems to take so long in coming. Even with snow still

Male and female flowers
of American Hazelnut

on the ground, the sight of Hazelnut flowers seems to mark the inevitable triumph of warmth over the persistence of cold.

Hazelnuts are most often found in the understory of older forests, in clearings, or along woodland borders. The plants usually grow in small clusters that have been produced by the growth of underground stems from a main central plant. These clusters may in turn be grouped together and form huge stands with very few other types of shrubs mixed in. A large stand of Hazelnuts takes a very long time to develop, for a clone started from a single seed, even after thirty years' growth, may cover an area of only two square meters.

Hazelnuts as a genus are easy to distinguish from other genera of shrubs. This is especially true in winter, for only five genera of shrubs have catkins on them throughout the winter months—*Myrica* (Sweet Gale), *Comptonia* (Sweet Fern), *Rhus* (Fragrant Sumac), *Alnus* (Alder), and *Corylus* (Hazelnut). Of these, only the winter catkins of Alder and Hazelnut hang downward, and while Alder catkins are a dark red-brown color, those of Hazelnut are beige.

Two signs of insect activity can be found on Hazelnut during the winter. Often you will see its catkins bent sharply up at their tips, making them look like the letter "J." If you open them carefully at their bend, you will find that they are hollowed out and may even discover a small insect larva inside

§ 26 §

the chamber. To the best of my knowledge, the maker of this gall has not yet been identified. The other evidence of insect work is called the Hazel Catkin Gall, formed by a gall gnat, *Cecidomyia squamicula*. The gall appears as a swelling of the basal scales of the catkin, while the rest of the catkin remains its normal size. The gnat is a close relative of the makers of the three common galls on Willow.

The two species of Hazelnut growing in eastern North America are most easily distinguished by their fruits. You may have trouble finding these nuts, which are covered by green leafy bracts called involucres and are usually hidden beneath the horizontal layers of leaves. While the actual fruits of the two American species are quite similar—both types measure about three quarters of an inch in diameter—their involucres are very different. The involucre of the American Hazelnut surrounds the nut and curls back at the tip, where its edges are frayed. The involucre of the Beaked Hazelnut extends beyond the nut for a half inch or more, forming a tube or beak. In this species, it is also covered with stiff, tiny hairs that

Winter catkins of Beaked Hazelnut, some deformed by gall-makers

can become lodged in your skin, like the fibers of steel wool or fiberglass. This covering may be a protective device of the fruits, and it certainly makes me have second thoughts before handling them.

Although fruits may be produced on a seedling as early as its second year, larger harvests occur much later in its life. A plant six to fifteen years old in full sun may produce eight or more fruits in a year, and pure stands of American Hazelnuts in southern climates have been found to produce three thousand fruits per acre. From my experience, a harvest of this size would be highly unusual in the north.

Composed of about 25 percent protein, 60 percent fat, and only 5 to 10 percent carbohydrate, hazelnuts have extremely good nutritional value.

Fruits of Hazelnut: lower left, Beaked Hazelnut; at right, American Hazelnut

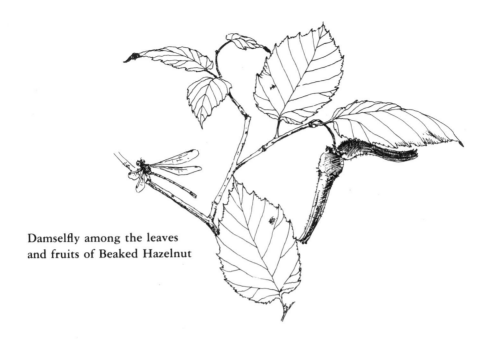

Damselfly among the leaves
and fruits of Beaked Hazelnut

This proportion of protein and fat to carbohydrate is better than that of either beechnuts or acorns; consequently, Hazelnuts in productive years can be an important source of wildlife food.

Check around the bases of Hazelnut plants in late summer and fall and you may find bits of the nut husks. If you look closely at these remains, you will undoubtedly see pairs of tooth marks left by the various rodents that feast on these nuts. The main consumers are Squirrels, Chipmunks, and Mice, and by comparing different tooth-mark sizes, you may get some clue as to which of these animals has been foraging. I have found some nuts actually eaten and hollowed out while still on the plant. This is most likely the work of a mouse, for only it is light enough to be supported by the fine branches.

If you follow the progress of the ripening nuts in summer, you may be lucky enough to harvest some before the woodland rodents do. This can be a real trick, for animals generally watch the plants more closely than you do. When I find a nut, I like to just eat it right then and there, but you may want to take some home and roast them briefly in the oven first. The nut

§ 29 §

meat is easy to extract: it is in large parts, much like the meat of butternuts, and not divided up into a network of compartments, like that of black walnuts and hickory nuts. Hazelnuts are the American cousin of the foreign Filbert and, in general, are overlooked by humans as a wild food treat in the woods.

I will never forget an experience I had when I first learned how to recognize Hazelnut. Somehow, I had always assumed that Hazelnut was a plant of a bygone era, something that had been used by the American Indians and early settlers, but that was no longer to be found. After seeing its leaf shape pictured in a book, I decided to go out and look for it. I chose an area that I knew well, with the hope that I might be able to locate at least one sample. No sooner had I started my walk than I found my first Hazelnut, right at the side of the path. I felt pleased to have discovered what I thought was a rare plant. But a few yards ahead there were more Hazelnuts, and I began to wonder just how common the plant was. I stepped off the trail and into the woods to see if it grew there as well. I soon realized that, for as far as I could see, the whole forest understory was primarily Hazelnuts. I was amazed by the extent of both the plant and my ignorance, and even today, still wonder how I overlooked for so long such a common and interesting wild plant.

ALDER

Alnus

ORDER: *Fagales.*   FAMILY: *Corylaceae.*   GENUS: *Alnus.*
SPECIES: *A. crispa,* Mountain Alder; *A. rugosa,* Speckled Alder;
A. serrulata, Common Alder; *A. maritima,* Seaside Alder.

OFTEN WHILE EXPLORING stream and swamp edges, you may suddenly notice water seeping up around the tops of your shoes. As you back out of the ooze, take a quick glance around you—it is likely that there will be Alders in the vicinity. Wet, spongy areas between open water and dry land are their favorite haunt. From the safety of higher ground, you can see that Alders are large shrubs, six to fifteen feet tall, and except for the fact that many trunks usually grow from the same spot, they often look like small trees. The easiest way to distinguish Alders from other woody plants is to look for the small clusters of fruits at the tips of the branches: they are dark brown, about three quarters of an inch long, and look like tiny pine cones.

Alders are important to the areas where they grow for a number of reasons. One is that their roots create dense mats that help hold soil in place. Alder roots also enrich the soil, for in association with certain bacteria, they absorb atmospheric nitrogen and make it available to neighboring plants. Although not well known for this ability, they are as productive in this regard as many commercial legume crops. Once established, Alders also spread rapidly by vegetative growth, either by sprouting new shoots from the base of older plants, by sending up shoots from underground stems, or by layering, a process in which a branch that has come in contact with the earth sends down roots and sends up shoots. Wherever you find Alders, they will usually be growing in small groves.

In summer, Alder groves provide cool, leafy cover for birds and mammals. Muskrats, Moles, and Shrews often have networks of trails and tunnels on the ground beneath the shrubs, while Red-winged Blackbirds and

ALDER

American Goldfinches build their nests in the fluttering leaves of the branches above. I have often waited near Alders to watch Goldfinches at work. Their nests are quite distinct, being small, compactly made with downy fibers, and hollowed out into a neat cup. In addition to the excitement of watching birds, the setting is always beautiful, the heat of the late summer sun offset by the moist coolness that drifts up from underneath the shady Alders.

In the wet areas where Alders thrive, a host of other plants join them, and since Alders have no colorful fruits or fragrant flowers, they are often overlooked in favor of their flashier companions. In spring, we would

Alder growing in its favored habitat

Nest of American Goldfinch
in the branches of Alder

probably first notice the Irises, in summer the Tearthumbs and Purple Loosestrife, in fall the Goldenrods and Joe-Pye Weed. But in winter, when all these plants die back, Alder is likely to attract our attention, not only because of its conelike fruits, but also because of the buds of the male and female flowers which dot the tips of its branches. The flowers are in the form of catkins, closed in winter but ready to expand in spring. The male catkins are red-brown and about an inch long. When in bloom, they expand and hang like long tassels in the wind. The pollen matures a little at a time, and instead of falling directly out of the catkin, collects in little cuplike sections of the flowers. When there is sufficient wind, the pollen is blown out and, with a little luck, carried to a female flower. The female catkins are very different in appearance. They are small and shaped like miniature pine cones. When they are in bloom, minute reddish hairs project from them in all directions to help catch the pollen grains out of the air. The female catkins are usually found immediately above the male catkins.

Alder is the only eastern shrub with both male and female catkins visible on its winter twigs. This is not true for all its species, however. Only Common Alder and Speckled Alder, both of which bloom in early spring before their leaves emerge, have catkins of both sexes during the cold

§ 33 §

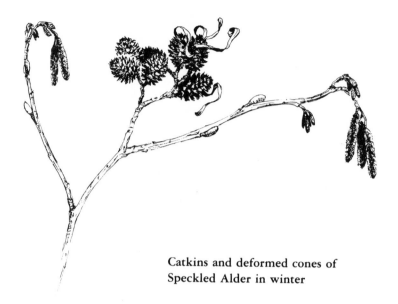

Catkins and deformed cones of
Speckled Alder in winter

months. Mountain Alder has only male catkins showing in winter; its female catkins grow in spring and bloom in summer. Our last native species, Seaside Alder, has no catkins at all in winter, but grows them in summer and does not bloom until early fall.

Alder fruits are also easily found on the plants in winter. If you take one and shake it into your hand, you are likely to see a few small dark-brown seeds drop out. They are eaten by Chickadees and Goldfinches. It is interesting to note that only the seed of the northern species, Mountain Alder, has two papery wings attached to either side. These wings have undoubtedly evolved to help disperse the seed by catching the wind. Many other woody plants in the far north rely on wind for both pollination and seed dispersal, possibly because there are fewer animals in the region to carry out these processes.

Some Alder cones have a few scales which have become elongated, making the whole fruit look like a woody flower. This distortion is caused by a fungus which is thought to grow mainly in the twigs. At one stage of their development, the elongated scales of the cones turn powdery white, a sign that the fungus is fruiting and releasing spores.

In spring, take time to look for some lovely little beetles that enjoy eating the leaves of Alders. Plants where the beetles have been feeding are easy to spot—the leaves will have many small holes in them. Two of the more common beetles that feed on Alders belong to the family *Chrysomelidae,* or Leaf-eating Beetles. One, the Alder Fleabeetle, *Altica bimarginata,* is only a quarter of an inch long, and a shiny steel blue. The other, *Lina interupta,* is about twice as long, and has a marvelous pattern of yellow and black on its back. The adult beetles overwinter on the ground beneath the leaves; in spring, they crawl into the Alders, feed on the new leaves, and lay eggs. The eggs hatch into small, dark-colored, flattened grubs which also feed on the leaves. When the larvae are mature, they pupate while attached by one end to the undersurface of the leaf. By looking under the leaves of a bush with larvae on it, you can find these pupae, which usually move a little when touched.

From late summer into fall, large masses of aphids congregate on the

Woolly Aphids and
Wanderer Butterfly
on Alder

stems of Alders to live off the sap of the plant. They are called Alder Blight Aphids, *Prociphilus tessellatus,* and because they exude a by-product of the sap through numerous pores on their backs, producing what looks like a mass of sticky cotton, they are commonly referred to as Woolly Aphids. The cottony excretions make the insects easy to spot. Earlier in the summer, the Woolly Aphids lived on the leaves of the Red Maple.

Among groves of Alders infested with Woolly Aphids, you may catch a glimpse of a small orange and brown butterfly flitting about. This butterfly is the Wanderer, *Feniseca tarquinius,* and it has a special relationship to the Woolly Aphids. The Wanderer may land under the aphids on twigs where their honeydew secretions have dripped and feed on this residue; at other times, it lands directly on the aphids and darts quickly across them, laying its eggs among the insects. The larva hatches and feeds on the bodies of the aphids, at the same time making a covering for itself out of silk and the empty skins of its prey. The larva takes only ten days to mature; when fully grown, it leaves the aphids and pupates on a leaf nearby. In a single year, the Wanderer may have up to three broods in the north and as many as five in the south. The butterfly is widespread in the eastern half of North America, but remains near both its adult and larval source of food. Our only species of the genus *Feniseca,* the Wanderer is also our only carnivorous butterfly larva.

OAK

Quercus

ORDER: *Fagales.*   FAMILY: *Fagaceae.*   GENUS: *Quercus.*
SPECIES: *Q. prinoides,* Chinquapin Oak; *Q. ilicifolia,* Scrub Oak.

ALTHOUGH WE ARE accustomed to thinking of Oaks as tall trees, two species in eastern North America—Chinquapin Oak and Scrub Oak—remain small and are considered shrubs. Both are found in dry, rocky, or sandy soil, especially at the edges of harsh environments such as along the coast or near mountaintops. Why these two species never grow taller than about fifteen feet is a puzzle that has not yet been solved. In any case, we can be glad that their growth is limited, for by presenting at eye level what would otherwise always be high in the treetops overhead, these smaller species enable us to study easily the botany of Oaks.

All Oaks can be divided into two groups, based upon the shapes of their leaves and the length of time their acorns require to mature. The Red Oak group is characterized by bristle tips on the lobes of its leaves and acorns that take two full summers to mature. The White Oak group has smooth edges to its leaves; its acorns mature in one summer. While we have only two shrub Oak species, it is interesting that each is in a different category, the Scrub Oak in the Red Oak group and the Chinquapin Oak in the White Oak group.

The specific names of the shrub Oaks describe the shapes of their leaves. Scrub Oak is the species *ilicifolia,* which means "leaves like holly." Its leaves are small with just a few pointed lobes, each tipped with short bristles —characteristics that make the leaves look like those of American Holly. The specific name of the Chinquapin Oak is *prinoides,* which reflects the fact that this species resembles *Quercus prinus,* or Chestnut Oak. Both these Oaks have ovate leaves with many large, rounded teeth along their edges.

§ 37 §

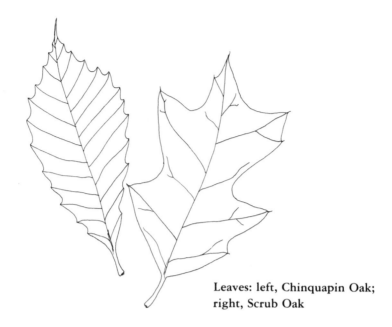

Leaves: left, Chinquapin Oak;
right, Scrub Oak

The name Chinquapin is believed to derive from the Algonquin Indian word *chincomen,* which meant "large fruit" and was originally applied to the shrub species of Chestnut, *Castanea pumila,* whose leaves resemble those of the oak.

Where I grew up, a brown fluffy material used to fill the gutters every year in late spring. As I walked home from school, I shuffled my feet through the fluff and had fun collecting it into large dust balls. I never wondered then what it was or where it came from. It wasn't until many years later that my adult curiosity caught up with my childhood experience and shed new light on it. I learned that these brown filaments cluttering the street were the male flowers of the Oaks, shed from the trees after they had released their pollen. When they open, the flowers are green, about two inches long, and they hang in tassel-like groups off the branches. They emerge in spring just as the leaves start to expand. The female flowers of Oaks will be found farther back on the same twigs. Though you will probably never see them on the tree species, for the flowers are too small and too high overhead, you do have a good chance of discovering them on the shrub species. They are reddish-brown buds, one quarter of an inch

§ 38 §

long, with a hairlike pistil at their tips. The pistil is divided in two, with each half curling back.

The female flowers of the Chinquapin Oak develop into acorns by the fall of the same year in which they bloom, but in the Scrub Oak they change only slightly during their first year, and not until the following fall do they ripen into mature acorns. In fall, you should be able to see two types of acorns on the Scrub Oak—the mature fruits on the older branches and the immature ones on the younger twigs. These immature acorns do not look like acorns at all; rather, they are just small, hardened buds. The key to recognizing them is to look for the remnants of the hairlike pistil protruding from their tip.

Acorns are one of our most important fall and winter wildlife foods. One of the shrub Oaks' benefits is that they provide acorns for mammals that either don't climb into trees or are too heavy to crawl out on small limbs. These include Deer, Bears, and Raccoons. Squirrels, the main consumers

Male flowers
of Chinquapin Oak
in spring

of acorns, can easily reach them, wherever the nuts are located. The Gray Squirrel and the Fox Squirrel bury their nuts singly, about two inches under the soil, and then retrieve them through the winter. The few acorns that are never retrieved are obviously in a perfect position for sprouting the following spring.

Many birds also eat acorns, among them the Wood Duck, Ruffed Grouse, Common Grackle, and especially the Blue Jay. The Blue Jays in my area have learned to consume the nuts in a fascinating way. A Jay will hold the acorn to the branch with its foot, and with a few pecks at the cap, remove a triangular portion from the nut's circumference. The cap then comes off easily and the bird eats the nut. I often find these distinctive caps littering the ground under trees where the Blue Jays have been feeding.

The shrub Oaks also afford a close look at some of the hundreds of galls that occur on Oaks. While galls form on all parts of Oaks, the greatest variety are found on the twigs. Most of these are caused by tiny insects called Cynipids or Gall Wasps. Cynipid wasps are easily recognized: about the size of a pencil point, they have a very humped thorax and a bulbous abdomen. There is still much to be discovered about the life histories of

Winter twig of Scrub Oak
with tiny first-year
acorns and leaf buds

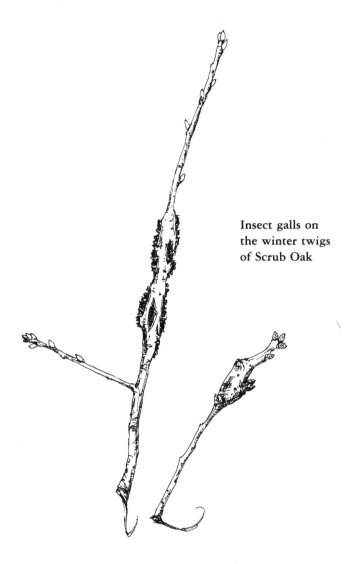

Insect galls on
the winter twigs
of Scrub Oak

these insects. It is known that each species creates a different shape of gall and always does so on the same part of the tree or shrub. Galls are easiest to see in winter, and I usually collect a few to keep on my desk. In the heat of the house, they often hatch, so that by late winter I often find little groups of wasps walking on the windows or flying about my lamp.

DUTCHMAN'S-PIPE

Aristolochia

ORDER: *Aristolochiales.*   FAMILY: *Aristolochiaceae.*
GENUS: *Aristolochia.*
SPECIES: *A. durior,* Dutchman's-pipe;
A. tometosa, Woolly Pipe Vine.

TWO NORTH AMERICAN species of vine belong to the genus *Aristolochia.* One has woolly stems and leaves and is called Woolly Pipe Vine; the other, with smooth leaves and stems, is called Dutchman's-Pipe. Both species are prominent in the southeastern quarter of the continent, and their unique fruits and flowers make them easily distinguished from all other vines. The flower, in bloom from May through June, is brown and looks like the bowl of a Dutch pipe. The fruit, which matures in fall and often hangs on the plant through winter, is cylindrical and measures two to three inches long. Even in late winter, when no fruits may be present, *Aristolochia* is easy to identify: it is the only twining vine with clusters of short twigs projecting off the main stem.

The generic name, *Aristolochia,* is a combination of two Greek words: *aristos,* meaning "best," and *lochos,* meaning "childbirth." This description, "best childbirth," probably does not refer to Dutchman's-Pipe, but to a herbaceous member of the same genus, *A. serpentaria,* commonly called Birthwort or Virginia Snakeroot. In the past, it was thought that chewing the roots of this plant eased some of the pains of childbirth. Another theory accounting for the name is based on the Doctrine of Signatures, a medieval theory stating that if any part of a plant looked like some other object, it was supposed to be associated with it and could aid in some way. Since the flower of Dutchman's-Pipe looked like a fetus, it was believed to help in childbirth.

Aristolochia grows rapidly, reaching heights of thirty feet or more and

DUTCHMAN'S-PIPE

producing a dense foliage of large, heart-shaped leaves that creates a deep shade on the ground below. These properties, and its unusual flowers, make *Aristolochia* a frequent choice for planting near porches or trellises. As a result, you may find the plant in the north, growing outside its natural range.

For the greater part of my life, I never once wondered about the form and function of flowers: I had seen Snapdragons, Buttercups, and Dandelions and never asked why they had different shapes or colors. Why did some smell nice and others not at all? I had never even asked the question, Why do plants have flowers? I now know that most of these questions can be answered by taking time to watch a flower, seeing what is attracted to it, and observing what it does after it arrives.

If you wished to study closely the flower of Dutchman's-Pipe, you would best choose May or June for your watch. In time, you would see small gnats or flies come to the mouth of the flower and crawl in. Strangely, you would not see them come out, at least not for a few hours or, in some cases, even for a few days. You might think they had died, but if you put your ear next to the bloom, you would probably hear them buzzing about inside. Your next observation, in the next day or two, would be that the mouth of the flower had wilted slightly; soon after, you would see the flies emerge, just as healthy as when they went in.

The first question that comes to mind is, Why did the flies remain in the flower so long? Perhaps an even more basic question would be, Why did they come to the flower at all? Insects are attracted to flowers for three reasons: to obtain food, to find a place to lay their eggs, or to find a mate.

Flower and pollinator of Dutchman's-Pipe. Redrawn from *The Mysteries of the Flowers* by Herbert Waldron Faulkner.

DUTCHMAN'S-PIPE

The flower of Dutchman's-Pipe is purple-brown at its entrance, and like many other flowers of this color (such as Skunk Cabbage or Pitcher Plant), it attracts small flies that lay their eggs in decaying animal matter. Some other members of the *Aristolochia* genus even give off bad odors, further suggesting their similarity to rotting flesh. Once inside the flower, however, the flies find no decaying material, and so buzz about trying to escape. They can't get out through the narrow passageway they used to enter, because it is lined with hairs that all point inward. When they fly to the inner part of the flower, they come in contact with the receptive female stigma. If they had previously been to another Dutchman's-Pipe flower, they are now carrying its pollen on their bodies, and as they attempt to escape, some of this pollen rubs off on the stigma of their present host. Once the stigma has received pollen from another flower, a new chain of events occurs. Pollen develops on anthers located near the stigma and falls down into the bowl, where the trapped insects can't avoid getting it on their legs, bodies, or wings. Soon after the pollen is produced, the mouth of the flower wilts slightly and the hairs that blocked the entrance become limp. The insects can now fly out, and at least a few will be attracted to other flowers and repeat the process.

Clearly, some flies will enter the flower without pollen and will have to remain in the flower until a pollen carrier arrives. Because it is in the flower's best interests to keep these potential future pollinators alive, it secretes some nectar, which the flies live on during their forced stay. Although it may seem strange that a fly would visit another flower after going through this ordeal, its actions are, of course, based not on reason but on instinct, and it is to these fixed instincts that the flower has evolved.

Once fertilized, the flowers develop into long fruits about the size and shape of a Cattail seedhead. The fruit, when mature, splits open vertically in a number of places. This splitting is unusual in that it occurs mostly at the upper portion of the fruit where it is attached to the vine, while the bottom portion of the fruit remains fused. The thin, flat seeds are stacked inside the capsule like saucers, and are dispersed by being shaken out.

Closely paralleling the range of the Dutchman's-Pipe is that of one of our more beautiful Swallowtail butterflies: the Blue Swallowtail, *Papilio philenor,* sometimes called the Pipe Vine Swallowtail, because of its close

§ 44 §

Fruit of Dutchman's-Pipe

Pipe-vine Swallowtail
and leaves and flower
of Dutchman's-Pipe

DUTCHMAN'S-PIPE

relationship to this plant. It lays groups of eggs on Dutchman's-Pipe leaves; when hatched, the larvae feed together at the leaf edges. As they mature, they become more independent and forage more on their own. The caterpillars, dark brown with thick spines along their backs, form a pupa typical of all Swallowtails—a chrysalis held against a twig in a sling made of a single thread. The adult butterfly is dark blue. The top of its wings are shaded with metallic green, while below they are dotted with bright orange and white spots. It is an interesting fact that the closest relatives of both this Swallowtail species and Dutchman's-Pipe live in the West Indies and South America, suggesting that the butterfly and the vine have slowly extended their range to the north.

In spring and summer, look for the Blue Swallowtail flying about Dutchman's-Pipe as it searches for suitable places to lay its eggs. You may also see it in fall, not at Dutchman's-Pipe, but at other plants in bloom, where it is feeding on nectar. The Swallowtail spends the autumn months storing up food, for it often overwinters as an adult.

SHRUB-YELLOWROOT

Xanthorhiza

ORDER: *Ranales.*　　FAMILY: *Ranunculaceae.*
GENUS: *Xanthorhiza.*
SPECIES: *X. simplicissima,* Shrub-Yellowroot.

ONE AFTERNOON, while traveling in the Smoky Mountains, I took some time to sit on a dry rock in the middle of a rushing stream. Water crashed over big boulders all around me, and its sound was all I could hear. On either side of the stream were small flat areas of sand bordered by eroded dark soil banks. These were clearly miniature flood plains, indicating that the water level rose substantially higher in certain seasons. While scanning these areas, I noticed a scattering of foot-high woody stems, each topped with a cluster of celery-like leaves. I waded to the bank to examine the plants and only when I was within a few feet of them did I realize that they were in bloom. Using a guidebook, I discovered they were a patch of Shrub-Yellowroot. It was the first time I had ever seen this plant growing in the wild.

My experience reveals a great deal about the habits of Shrub-Yellowroot. First, it grows best in very wet areas, typically the flood plains of streams and rivers. In such environments, it spreads with an extensive root system that sends up many new shoots. These often form small clusters of the plant, which, along with the root system, undoubtedly help to hold the soil together during the temporary spring flooding of their habitat. Other possible adaptations that might help the plant reduce its resistance to the force of water during flooding are its lack of branching, its flexible stem, and its short height.

A lack of branches limits the methods a plant can use to arrange its leaves in light. Shrub-Yellowroot solves this problem in two ways. First, it grows

SHRUB-YELLOWROOT

all leaves from its end bud, arranging them in a circular pattern similar to a rosette; second, it has compound leaves with long petioles, which maximize their potential for collecting light energy. To support the added weight of the compound leaves, the base of the leaf petiole is widened and attached firmly to the stem.

On Shrub-Yellowroots you will notice two types of scars. One is a compact set of encircling rings, signs of where the end-bud scales were attached. By counting the number of sets, you can determine the age of the plant, for each set of rings indicates a new year of growth. Between the sets of bud scale scars are more widely spaced scars, each almost encircling the stem. These are the leaf scars, where leaves from previous years were attached to the stem.

In spring, the flowers of this species emerge from the end bud before the leaves. As I discovered in my encounter near the stream, the flowers are so inconspicuous that they are easily overlooked. They are purple to brown, about a half inch in diameter, and borne on long racemes. They have no scent, and their only notable feature is the dots of yellow pollen at their centers. Generally, if a flower that does not smell displays its pollen prominently, it is pollinated by insects that come only to feed on pollen, rather than nectar. Yet I have patiently watched the flower of Shrub-Yellowroot, and except for a few gnats, I have seen very few insect visitors. Since

Stonefly on leaf of Shrub-Yellowroot

Flowers of Shrub-Yellowroot
in spring

there are no written records of how the blossoms of this plant are pollinated, the mechanism remains a mystery.

On the shores of the mountain stream, Shrub-Yellowroot grew out of clumps of earth that were higher than the surrounding shore. The earth was held together by masses of fine roots. I dug slightly into these and found rhizomes, a quarter of an inch in diameter, connecting the separate aerial stems. I happened to scrape one as I was digging and immediately realized how the plant got its name: the wood just under the bark of the roots or stems is bright yellow. The Latin generic name, *Xanthorhiza*, has the same meaning as the common name—*xantho* meaning "yellow" and *rhiza* meaning "root." The lovely specific name, *simplicissima*, probably refers to the plant's lack of branching. A friend once pointed out that at least some of the people who assigned the scientific names to plants were sensitive to the beauty as well as to the descriptive nature of the names they created. Ever since then, I have kept a mental record of my favorite scientific plant names. Certainly *Xanthorhiza simplicissima* is one of them.

The fruits that develop from Shrub-Yellowroot's flowers usually contain only one mature seed each. These fruits are described as follicles, a classification indicating that they have a non-fleshy casing that splits along one

§ 49 §

side. In this respect they are similar to the fruits of Spirea and Milkweed. The seeds are enclosed in small inflated capsules which help keep them afloat, enabling them to be dispersed by the water. Clearly there must be other ways of dispersal as well, or else how could the plants spread to areas upstream?

Shrub-Yellowroot typically has as its neighbors other woody plants that favor the banks of streams. When I first encountered the plant by the mountain stream, it was in the company of Sycamores, Ironwoods, Azaleas, and Alders. Among these companions, Shrub-Yellowroot is one of the "quieter" members, never particularly conspicuous in any season. Perhaps this unobtrusiveness is one of its charms; you have to go looking for the plant, and having made the search, you enjoy the discovery all the more.

Fruits of Shrub-Yellowroot in winter

BARBERRY

Berberis

ORDER: *Ranales.*   FAMILY: *Berberidaceae.*   GENUS: *Berberis.*
SPECIES: *B. canadensis,* American Barberry;
B. vulgaris, Common Barberry; *B. Thunbergii,* Japanese Barberry.

THERE ARE THREE common species of Barberry, easily differentiated by the arrangement of their berries. The so-called Common Barberry, introduced to this country from Europe, was brought there from the mountains of Asia. Its berries, in groups of ten to twelve, are borne on racemes. The other common introduced species is Japanese Barberry; its berries are borne singly right off the stem. Both introduced species are widely distributed, presumably by birds that eat the fruits and void the seeds in their droppings. The only native species in the East, American Barberry, has a range limited to the mountainous woods of Virginia and Georgia. Although its berries also grow in racemes, there tend to be only six or less berries per raceme.

Barberry is one of the few shrubs that has had laws enacted requiring its eradication. In Europe, farmers had been troubled for hundreds of years by a fungus (now known as *Pucinia graminis*) that attacked grain crops such as wheat, rye, oats, and barley. It was eventually noticed that only crops with Barberry growing near them were destroyed. In 1865, a man named Anton de Bary discovered that the fungus had two hosts—the grain crops in summer and Barberry in winter—and that both were necessary for the fungus to survive in cold climates. At this point, the Europeans enacted some trial laws that attempted to force landholders to remove Barberry if it was near a grain crop.

When early European settlers came to America, they brought European Barberry with them, possibly because the plant had been used in Europe

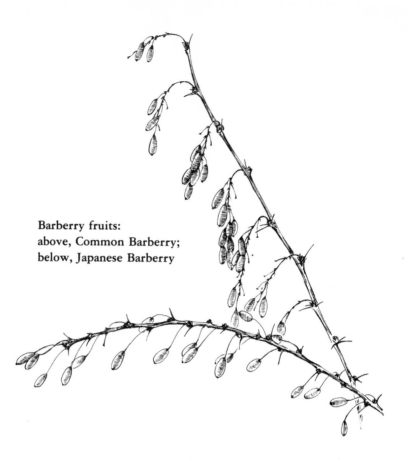

Barberry fruits:
above, Common Barberry;
below, Japanese Barberry

as a natural hedgerow or because its fruits were used for jellies. Some Barberry undoubtedly also came over by chance in the feed or droppings of cattle. The fungus came to North America with the plant and as early as 1660, wheat was being "blasted" by the fungus. Connecticut and Massachusetts were the first states to enact laws to rid the area of the plant, but they were ineffectual. The fungus soon spread to our only native species in the East, American Barberry.

It was soon discovered that the fungus did not require Barberry as its alternate host in warmer climates (such as our South), so that its spores, carried north in spring by wind, could still infect crops where Barberry had been eliminated. As a result, the fungus was and still is difficult to control.

§ 52 §

BARBERRY

Oddly, Japanese Barberry, a common ornamental, has proved to be immune to the fungus.

There are at least two good reasons to visit Barberry in spring. One is to taste its fresh green leaves; when chewed, they have a pleasant, acidic flavor, very similar to that of Sheep-Sorrel leaves. The other is to take a close look at the small yellow flowers that hang below its branches. Although they are not especially beautiful and their strong odor is not particularly pleasant, their pollination mechanism is one of the most fascinating of all our shrubs.

The female part of the Barberry flower, the pistil, is shaped like a small post in the flower's center. Surrounding the pistil, but spread away from it and pressed against each petal, are the male stamens. Nectar is located at the base of the stamens, so that when a bee sticks its mouth into the nectaries it triggers a mechanism that makes the stamens spring inward and press against the insect's mouth and head. As the bee pulls its head back, pollen brushes along the sides of its face. Each stamen can spring independently, so that the bee may be snapped upon as many as six times.

You can simulate the actions of the bee and see the floral mechanism

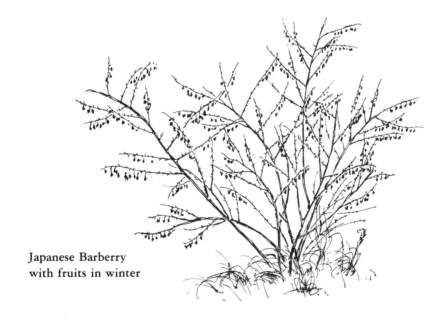

Japanese Barberry
with fruits in winter

work by taking a pin or fine pine needle and touching it gently to the base of the stamens. The stamen will turn in upon it; as you pull out the pin, look for pollen coating its tip. In some Barberry flowers, I have found that the stamens "reset" themselves and perform the whole trick over again in five to ten minutes. The flower is a marvelous little event, and once you experience it I guarantee you will come back to visit the plant each spring.

Barberry is easily identified in all seasons by its fine, sharp thorns and short spur twigs, both produced along basically unbranched stems. It typically grows a number of stems from the same spot. If you ever have an occasion to break off a stem or dig the plant up, you will discover a bright-yellow sap in its wood. This has been used to make a yellow dye for coloring cloth or wool.

Examine the branching pattern of Barberry in winter, or in early spring, when the leaves are just emerging. The stems are usually long, arching, and unbranched and grow short spurs from which all the leaves are produced. Every year, a new set of leaves is grown from these spurs. Although the

Flowers of Common Barberry

Branching patterns of Barberry
showing spurs and long twigs

spurs elongate only a fraction of an inch each season, the tips of the branches may grow by as much as a foot.

In shady areas, you are likely to find an unusual branching pattern in Barberry: a spur bearing leaves at the tip of a long branch, an indication the branch has stopped its rapid growth and is now producing only the fraction-of-an-inch spur growth each season. Branch tips on older bushes sometimes change from terminal growth to spur growth and then back to terminal growth.

Besides being a tangy trail nibble, Barberry's leaves show an interesting pattern of growth. While the spurs originally emanate from every side of the branch, after a few years each turns upward so that all its leaves face the sun. The leaves are borne in rosettes in which each leaf varies in the size of its blade and the length of its petiole. This variety allows the entire rosette to present a more or less continuous surface to the light, with little

BARBERRY

or no overlap. This leaf arrangement is seen on many other shrubs, but it is particularly obvious in Barberry.

The berries from Barberry make a good jam, some say one of the best to be had from wild fruits. If you taste one of the berries, I suggest that you do so just after they turn red, for later in the summer and fall they are relatively tasteless. The same advice holds true for the leaves, which become bitter later in the summer.

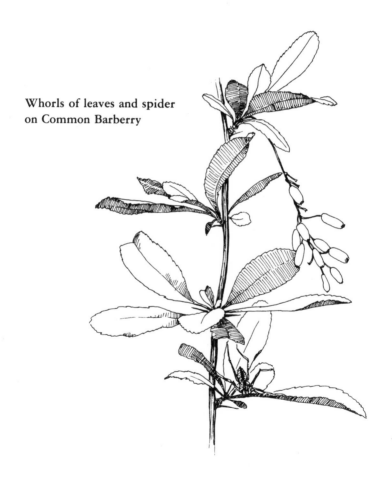

Whorls of leaves and spider
on Common Barberry

SWEETSHRUB

Calycanthus

ORDER: *Ranales.*   FAMILY: *Calycanthaceae.*   GENUS: *Calycanthus.*
SPECIES: *C. fertilis,* Smooth Sweetshrub;
C. floridus, Hairy Sweetshrub.

THE SWEETSHRUBS are native to deciduous forests in the southeastern United States and are especially common in the foothills of the Appalachian Mountains. Their paired and widely spaced branches, which form simple and elegant designs in the open understory, make the plants easy to recognize even from a distance. The common names of this species, Sweetshrub, Allspice, and Strawberry Shrub, come from the pleasant, volatile odor obtained by crushing one of the leaves or lightly scratching the bark. Some describe this scent as being like that of strawberries, but I find it quite different and unique. The two eastern species of the plants, Smooth Sweetshrub *(C. fertilis)* and Hairy Sweetshrub *(C. floridus)*, look very similar but can be distinguished by their flowers: those of Smooth Sweetshrub are very fragrant, while those of Hairy Sweetshrub have little or no odor.

Sweetshrub has one of the most unusual fruits of any of our common shrubs. When I first saw one on the plant, I had no idea it was the fruit and approached cautiously and with wonder. A shriveled dark-brown sac, about two inches long, was hanging off the branch; in size and shape, it reminded me of a Cecropia cocoon. As I removed it from the plant, I heard something rattle loosely inside. I again thought of a Cecropia cocoon, for when parasitized, it is filled with many tiny wasp pupae. I put the sac down on the ground and started to cut it open with a knife. The exterior split easily and had the texture of parchment. I pried apart the outer shell, somewhat apprehensive that I might discover some strange animal activity inside. To my surprise, the casing was filled with loose brown seeds that, in color and shape, looked much like baked beans.

§ 57 §

SWEETSHRUB

Because the seeds of Sweetshrub are often found loose in their casing, one might wonder how they developed with no apparent connection to the plant. But if you open some seed cases carefully, you will find the seeds still attached to the sides of the casing, receiving their nourishment. These attachments will eventually dry out and break. The individual seeds, which are technically achenes, are covered with fine silky hairs, and have a delicate and pleasant odor when crushed.

Sweetshrub fruits may remain attached to the branches for more than a year and so may be found on the plant in any season. One spring, when I was opening one of the fruits to look at the seeds inside, a horde of small ants streamed out onto my hands, carrying what were either eggs or the pupal cases of their young. It seemed to me a highly unusual place for an ant nest and I left with many puzzling questions, all of which can be answered only through further exploration.

Fruits of Sweetshrub:
below, opened to show seeds

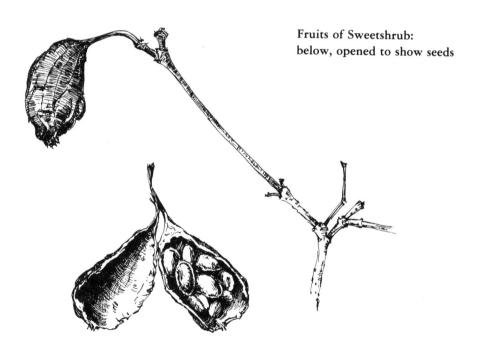

Flowers of Sweetshrub

The generic name of Sweetshrub means "cup flower" and most likely refers to the large, hollow receptacle beneath the petals of the flower, in which the seeds develop. This "cup" eventually expands into the tough covering for the fruits. In fact, at the tip of the matured fruit you can still see scars at the points where the petals once were attached.

Even a brief glance at Sweetshrub's flower, with its many burgundy, straplike petals curving in at their tips, reveals how strikingly different this flower is from those of other shrubs. Although the pollination strategies of the eastern species have not yet been studied, that of a similar western species, *C. occidentalis,* has been examined closely. Because the flowers of the eastern shrubs seem to have a similar strategy, I will describe the research on the western species so that you may have some clues for your own exploration.

There are basically two stages in the blooming of the flowers of the western species. First, a few of the outer petals open out while at the same time the innermost petals curl inward, creating a passageway down to the matured stigmas of the flower. Beetles belonging to the family *Nitidulidae* —small, dark insects with the common name Sap-feeding Beetles—have been observed crawling down this passageway and becoming trapped inside the flower. As soon as one of these beetles gets pollen from another flower onto the receptive stigmas, the flower goes into its second stage. In it, a few sterile stamens fold down over the stigmas, possibly protecting them from being eaten, and fertile stamens shed pollen on the beetles, still trapped inside the flower. At this point, the flower turns brown and loses its scent, and the petals and sepals open. The beetles, dusted with fresh pollen, can now escape and visit another flower. This marvelous method for cross-pollination is quite similar to that used by Dutchman's-Pipe. The beetles that are among the pollinators of the western species are common in the East as well.

A notable difference between the two eastern species is that while Smooth Sweetshrub has little or no odor but produces many fruits, Hairy Sweetshrub has very fragrant flowers but generally produces very few fruits. This would lead one to believe that the species producing more fruits either has a more successful method of attracting pollinators than odor, or else is often self-pollinated.

Millions of years ago, when the angiosperms (our modern flowers) were first developing, the most common pollinators of today (flies and bees) had not yet evolved. It is believed that primitive angiosperm flowers were pollinated either by passive elements, such as the wind, or by active agents, such as beetles, which were especially common at the time. These primitive flowers shared a number of characteristics: a lack of marked differences in the structure of sepals, petals, and stamens—a large, open form—and a pollination method of "mess and soil," whereby an insect became covered with pollen by merely crawling over the flower. These last two characteristics are believed to be adaptations to pollination by beetles. The flowers of Sweetshrub, which have all these characteristics, may seem unusual to us in that their primitive form is such a contrast to the more modern flowers of our other common shrubs.

SPICEBUSH

Lindera

ORDER: *Ranales.*   FAMILY: *Lauraceae.*   GENUS: *Lindera.*
SPECIES: *L. Benzoin,* Spicebush.

As YOU WALK through a grove of Spicebush in early spring, you may not consciously notice the shrubs' flowers. Although their color and odor are inconspicuous, the flowers will have their effect, working quietly on your senses and creating in you a rich feeling of the coming of spring and the renewal of growth. Spicebush is one of the earliest fragrant shrub flowers to bloom in the new year, preceded only by the Willows. The blossoms, which appear on the bare twigs long before the leaves, are yellow, arranged in tight little clusters, and have a subtle but pungent odor. The flowers are unisexual and the sexes occur on separate plants. They have no petals but advertise their presence with six yellow sepals and their lemony fragrance. Spicebush's blooms can be so plentiful that from a distance they appear as a light haze in the spring woods.

Among the many insects that come to collect either the pollen or the nectar of Spicebush are solitary bees, numerous species of flies, and small beetles, including various types of Ladybird Beetles. One of the visiting flies resembles a Bumblebee except that it has a very long extended mouth-part that enables it to hover in front of the flower like a Hummingbird as it sips nectar. This insect is commonly known as a Bee Fly. A member of the family *Bombyliidae,* it has an active adult phase that lasts for only a few weeks in early spring.

It is amazing how often Spicebush is found growing in exactly the same habitat—under a canopy of taller deciduous trees along the edge of an old river or stream. Spicebush seems to thrive in this moist environment, where hundreds of years of seasonal flooding have gradually deposited a soil that

Spicebush flowers

is moderately acidic and high in organic content. You will rarely find the plant growing alone, for shortly after becoming established, it sends up new shoots off its spreading root system.

In early summer, look among Spicebush's leaves for some that are folded in half along their midrib. As you gently open them, you will find silk webbing close to the leaf surface, the work of the Spicebush Swallowtail caterpillar. It weaves an increasingly tighter webbing across the midrib of the leaf in such a way that the leaf folds. This fold becomes its protection during the periods when it is not feeding. The caterpillar has been observed to use generally three different leaves during the successive stages of its life. At some point, if you are fortunate, you will open a leaf and find the caterpillar inside. It is gray and watery-looking when young, but a spectacular leaf-green, with two large black and yellow spots on its back just behind its head, when mature. The spots look much like eyes and have probably evolved to frighten predators. Like many other Swallowtail larvae, it has a bright-orange organ on the top of its head. Though usually drawn within the body, this is extended and exudes a strong odor when the caterpillar is sufficiently disturbed. You can look for the caterpillar again in early fall, since this butterfly has two broods per year. It is in its pupal stage in midsummer and again in winter.

The adult Spicebush butterfly is a lovely, large, darkly colored insect with

§ 62 §

SPICEBUSH

projections called "tails" at the base of its hind wings. It will be seen flitting about the groves of Spicebush in late spring and late summer, sometimes alighting briefly on the leaves as it deposits its eggs. Look for the butterfly, the folded leaves, and the caterpillar on Sassafras as well as Spicebush, because both are used as host plants by the insect. Sassafras and Spicebush,

Adult Spicebush Swallowtail larva and folded leaf home of larva

Winter twig and buds of Spicebush

SPICEBUSH

both members of the family *Lauraceae,* are similar in their flower structure and in having aromatic twigs and leaves.

Every part of the Spicebush is fragrant. In winter, the twigs emit a pleasant odor when scratched; in spring, the small yellow blossoms have the same fragrance; in summer, the leaves when rubbed or crushed give off a spicy scent; and in fall, the fruits have an agreeable aroma. I find the fruits are the most pungent as well as the most beautiful part of the plant. By midsummer, they are full grown and bright green; in fall, as the leaves turn to golden yellow, the fruits ripen to a deep shiny red. Two of the main consumers of the fruits are the Wood Thrush and the Veery, two species which, like the plant, have evolved to living in moist deep woods.

Spicebush has also been called Snapwood, possibly because of its brittle twigs. These can be collected in winter and steeped in hot water for about fifteen minutes to make a fairly good tea. One way to identify Spicebush in winter is to look for its dark-green twigs dotted with groups of small round flower buds. But obviously, the most pleasant way to identify the plant in any season is to scratch its young twigs lightly and smell its marvelous spicy odor.

Fruits of Spicebush

GOOSEBERRY, CURRANT

Ribes

ORDER: *Rosales.*   FAMILY: *Saxifragaceae.*   GENUS: *Ribes.*
SPECIES: *R. hirtellum,* Smooth Gooseberry;
R. Grossularia, European Gooseberry; *R. lacustre,* Bristly Currant;
R. glandulosum, Skunk Currant;
R. americanum, American Black Currant,
R. nigrum, European Black Currant; and many others.

IN MANY AREAS of eastern North America, Currants and Gooseberries are not very common, and are found only in small isolated patches. Part of the reason for this sparseness is that these plants have been subject to a program of eradication since the early 1900s. The history of this program is intimately connected to the White Pine and the economic growth of the United States. The White Pine has been an extremely valuable tree to the economy of North America. Especially around 1900, when the country was growing rapidly, these trees were in tremendous demand for everything from houses to matchsticks. Our forest industry was then not large enough to meet the need for new seedling pines. Because the European forest industry was well developed, American foresters sent seeds overseas so that young plants could be started there and then be shipped back and grown into trees. But along with the returning seedlings was a fungus *(Cronartium ribicola)* called a blister rust that attacked and killed White Pine. Like many other rusts, it needed two hosts to complete its life cycle; its alternate host was various species of *Ribes.* The importing of seedling trees quickly reached mammoth proportions. In 1909, over ten million young plants were reported to have been brought into the country, and by 1915, the rust

§ 65 §

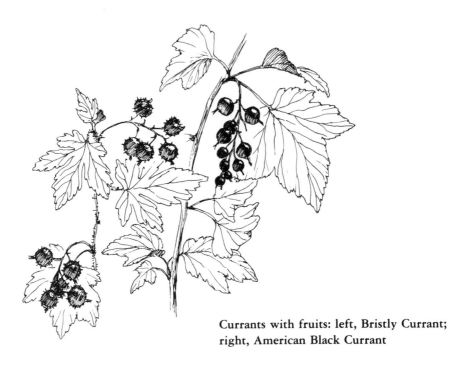

Currants with fruits: left, Bristly Currant; right, American Black Currant

was already seen attacking native stands of Pine. The Pine was so important that the only solution was to eliminate the alternate host, the Currants and Gooseberries. The destruction was carried out primarily in the important growing areas where the most White Pines were planted, with an obvious effect on the distribution and population of Currants and Gooseberries.

Currants and Gooseberries are generally low shrubs with long, sparsely branched stems. The stems are often arching, like those of Brambles. This trait, along with their habit of freely producing new aerial stems from spreading root systems, often causes the plants to form small thickets. The flowers of all species begin to bloom in early spring. They are small and inconspicuous, generally lightly colored with yellows and greens, although some are white or tinted with pink. Honeybees and Bumblebees are the main pollinators, possibly attracted by the slight fragrance produced by the blooms. The insects come to gather both pollen and nectar.

A number of differences between Currants and Gooseberries have led botanists in the past to place the two groups into separate genera. The main characteristic that has been used to divide the two groups is the structure

§ 66 §

of their pedicels, or the small stalk that attaches the fruit to the main flower stalk. In the Gooseberries, the pedicel is continuous with the rest of the of the main flower stalk. When the fruit is fully ripened, the pedicel breaks off and the fruit falls. Another difference between the two species is that the flowers of Gooseberry are borne in clusters of five or less, while those of Currants are borne in clusters of more than five and are arranged on graceful racemes.

Today, because their similarities are considered to outweigh their differences, the two groups are considered only subgenera of the genus *Ribes*. Although some characteristics, such as thorns, overlap the groups, Gooseberries generally have large thorns along their stems just beneath each leaf node, while the Currants are usually thornless. But just to confuse matters, there are Smooth Gooseberry, which is relatively thornless, and Bristly Currant, which is covered with dense bristles.

Currants have small, dark-colored fruits, while those of Gooseberry are larger, with duller colors. All the fruits of *Ribes* are tipped with the remains of the calyx from the flower. The use of the fruits by wildlife has been greatly affected by the eradication program. They are now of only minimal value to wildlife in the East, although in the West, where there are many more species, they are still important. Small mammals, such as Mice and Voles, tend to discard the pulp and gnaw into the seeds. Birds, the main dispersers of the plants, eat the whole fruit, and the seeds pass through their

Flowers of Prickly Gooseberry

systems. Tests done on the seeds of Gooseberry show that they germinate more readily after passing through the digestive system of certain species of birds.

Many European species of *Ribes* have been brought to North America, for the fruits are well loved in pies and jellies. Many of these plants have escaped from gardens and are now found growing wild, the most common being the European Gooseberry, the Garden Red Currant, and the European Black Currant. I have never had the chance to cook with the fruits of Currants or Gooseberries, but I have had plenty of opportunities to taste the results. A number of Gooseberry pies have passed my way within my lifetime and I have thoroughly enjoyed Currant jelly for both its taste and its deep color.

Fruits and leaves of Smooth Gooseberry

WITCH HAZEL

Hamamelis

ORDER: *Rosales.* FAMILY: *Hamamelidaceae.* GENUS: *Hamamelis.*
SPECIES: *H. virginiana,* Witch Hazel;
H. vernalis, Springtime Witch Hazel.

IF THERE IS only one time when you are able to visit Witch Hazel, make it the fall. If you arrive and find that the plant has just shed its leaves, that its branches are bare, and that it appears to have settled into its winter dormancy, then you are too early. Wait a week or two and return; you are likely to see the bare branches covered with spidery light-yellow blooms. Witch Hazel blooms later than any of our other wild shrubs and vines, at a time when most other woody plants have shed their leaves. Its flowering marks the end of fall, for once its blooms fade, the cold weather sets in and the colors of the woods no longer change with each day, but seem fixed, at least for the early part of winter.

Even though its flowers have disappeared, there are still good reasons for visiting Witch Hazel in winter. One is to find its marvelous seed capsules, which have required almost a full year to mature. They contain one or two shiny black seeds about the size and shape of rice grains. As the capsule dries, it splits across the top; the seeds, now under pressure, shoot out through the opening with an audible snap, and are dispersed five to ten feet from the parent plant.

Another interesting growth on the winter twigs, the Spiny Witch Hazel Gall, is not particularly easy to spot, for it is dark-colored and there are only a few on any given group of plants. It looks like a miniature pineapple and is caused by the aphid *Hamamelistes spinosus.* The female aphid irritates the flower bud, causing a gall to form, and then lays her eggs within. Winged adults emerge from the gall and fly to Birches, where the aphids go through three generations before returning to Witch Hazel. Some species of aphids

Witch Hazel flowers and opened seed pods,
also the Spiny Witch Hazel Gall

in the north have been observed never to migrate to Birches, but complete their entire life cycle on the Witch Hazel.

There are two species of Witch Hazel in eastern North America. One blooms in late fall after the leaves have shed; the other, sometimes known as Springtime Witch Hazel, blooms in late winter and early spring before the leaves appear. The latter species is more southern in range, the former is more northern. A question for which I have not been able to find an answer is, Who pollinates the flowers? Both species bloom at times when very few insects are out collecting food. I have watched the flowers when they are in bloom and the only visitors I have seen are ants.

In summer, the leaves of Witch Hazel are the main centers of activity. Here you will find a fascinating insect gall, shaped like a minute peak of meringue. The gall-maker, *Hormaphis hamamelidis,* is an aphid which in spring chews a hole through the undersurface of the leaf, causing a gall to form above. The eggs she lays within the gall soon hatch, and the young can be found crowded inside the gall in early summer. The aphids emerge and fly to Birch, where they pass through four generations, finally returning to Witch Hazel.

Two other signs of summer animal activity can be seen on Witch Hazel's leaves. You will notice that some leaves have been rolled into a tight cylinder for half their length, starting at the tip and progressing toward the petiole. This construction is the work of the larva of a Tortricid moth, *Cacoecia rosaceana.* The other occurrence will be seen at the base of Witch

WITCH HAZEL

Hazel leaves. Here the leaf is often folded over right along one of the side veins and carefully tied back to the rest of the leaf. The Witch Hazel Leaf Folder, *Episimus argutanus,* is a small moth whose larva makes this fold and then feeds on the inner layer of the leaf in the fold, causing it to turn brown. I find both of these very common and always done in exactly the same way.

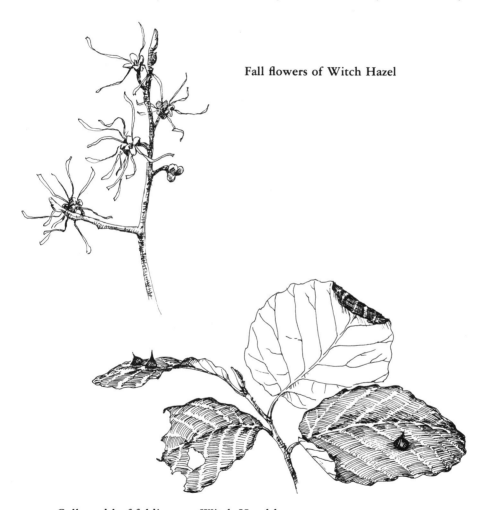

Fall flowers of Witch Hazel

Galls and leaf-foldings on Witch Hazel leaves

WITCH HAZEL

Witch Hazel is usually seen in sparse colonies of plants growing in the understory of dry or moist woods. This configuration results because the plant spreads by rootstocks that grow new aerial stems. Its companion plants include Hazelnut, Blueberry, Huckleberry, and Buckthorn. Witch Hazel grows slowly, and after reaching a height of about ten feet, projects almost all new growth in a lateral direction.

For hundreds of years, people have claimed that the oil from Witch Hazel bark can cure a variety of bodily ills. Even today you can buy oil of witch hazel at your local drugstore, mixed liberally with alcohol. I am not certain whether witch hazel oil relieves any of the aches and pains we get from civilization, but I am sure that the plant can provide a healthy diversion. If you take the time to observe its flowers, pods, seeds, leaf rollers, and galls, you will find it always a bewitching source of wonder in the woods.

Branching of Witch Hazel in the winter woods

NINEBARK

Physocarpus

ORDER: *Rosales.*　　FAMILY: *Rosaceae.*　　GENUS: *Physocarpus.*
SPECIES: *P. opulifolius,* Ninebark.

NINEBARK IS NOT a very common shrub. Because it does not form groves like many other shrubs, it is usually found only as a single specimen. Its most obvious characteristic is a thin, papery bark of varied colors that exfoliates off the base of its stems. Because the bark is looser and more ragged than that of any of our other common shrubs or vines, it is a good means of identifying Ninebark throughout the year.

The common name of *Physocarpus,* Ninebark, is believed to have been acquired when the plants were known for the number of medicinal cures they could effect. Ninebark would therefore clearly be better than Seven-bark (another name for Wild Hydrangea). The specific name of Ninebark, *opulifolius,* means "leaves like opulus," and refers to *Viburnum opulus,* an introduced species from Europe commonly called Guelder Rose. Its leaves are three-lobed—somewhat like those of a maple—and toothed around their edges. Ninebark leaves are very similar, and can be found in two slightly different forms, depending on which branch of the plant they grow on. Leaves on the main vegetative branches are quite large and have long lobes; leaves borne on the fruiting branches are smaller and sometimes have no lobes at all.

Take time to observe the interesting branching structure of Ninebark. The primary vegetative branches are long and arching, grow from the same spot, and tend to be crowded together. After a few years, they generate smaller fruiting branches off the sides of their newer growth. These produce flowers and fruits for several years and then die back. The fruiting branches are easily recognized; they are the thin pointed twigs with little knobs all along their tips.

Exfoliating bark of Ninebark

Ninebark flowers, which bloom in June, are arranged in a slightly rounded, umbel-like cluster. The configuration of individual flowers is five sepals, then five white to pink petals, and finally twenty to forty stamens attached to a nectar ring inside the flower. The stamens have long filaments that hold the anthers well out in front of the flower. This structure creates a generalized type of pollination mechanism, similar to that of Willows, whereby an insect landing on the flower cannot avoid brushing many of the anthers.

At the center of the Ninebark flower is its most interesting feature, a group of three swollen carpels, each tipped by a long style. Once the flowers are fertilized, the petals detach and the carpels begin to swell and gradually change from green to a lovely burgundy red. This is one of the plant's most beautiful stages, but it is easily overlooked because it is so short-lived. When finally mature, the swollen carpels are often still tipped by their styles. Around the base of the carpels are also remnants of the stamens—evidence of the flower's former structure. By fall, each carpel looks like a small inflated bellows; because of this characteristic, the plant has the generic name *Physocarpus,* which means bladder or bellows *(physa)* and fruit *(karpos).* The drooping fruit clusters are very obvious on the plants in fall after the leaves have been shed.

One winter, I went out to collect some Ninebark fruits for a closer examination. They had all been shed from the branches, so I picked them

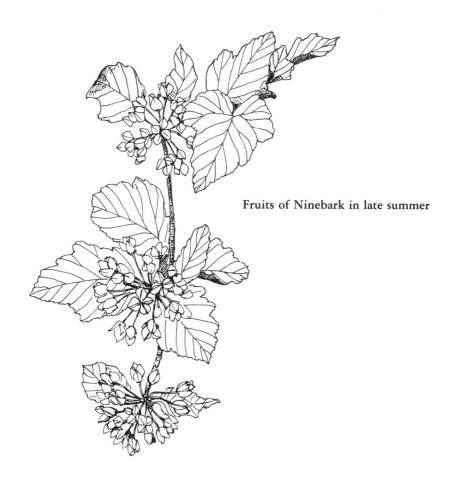

Fruits of Ninebark in late summer

Fruits and branching pattern of Ninebark in winter.

up off the snow beneath the plant. I left them on my desk to dry, and when I looked at them after a while, they seemed to be an entirely different shape from when I had brought them inside. A careful look revealed that each of the bellows-like carpels had split at its tip and opened out, making the three carpels in each separate fruit look like a small woody flower with cupped petals. I wondered if the carpels had opened because they had dried out inside, so I dipped them in water briefly. No sooner had I taken them out of the water than they were completely closed. I then tried to get them to open by drying them out, but not until much later did they fully open again. Try this experiment yourself; it is especially fun to see the carpels close after they have been dipped in water.

When Ninebark is in bloom, visit its flowers to look for insects. One insect that is very common on the blooms is the beetle called the Rose Chafer, *Macrodactylus subspinosus.* It is a light-yellow-to-beige beetle with

NINEBARK

long, sharply spined black legs. In the same family as the Japanese Beetle —*Scarabaeidae* or Scarabs—it can often be found in pairs, mating right on the blossoms. You may also find a few species of Long-horned Beetles of the family *Cerambycidae* on Ninebark flowers. Ninebark has a particularly good flower for beetles, since its umbel-like arrangement provides a large landing platform for these generally clumsy fliers and its pollen is very accessible to their chewing mouthparts.

Ninebark is one of my favorite plants to visit at least once in each season, to see, first, its emerging leaves, then its blooms and insects, then its ripening fruits, and finally, in winter, its beautiful exfoliating bark. If you find a Ninebark near you, start to observe it in all seasons and I am sure you will begin to feel as I do about this fascinating shrub.

Flowers of Ninebark
with Rose-chafer Beetle

SPIREA

Spiraea

ORDER: *Rosales.*   FAMILY: *Rosaceae.*   GENUS: *Spiraea.*
SPECIES: *S. alba,* Meadowsweet;
S. latifolia, Broad-leaved Meadowsweet;
S. tomentosa, Hardhack; *S. corymbosa,* Corymbed Spirea.

AT FIRST GLANCE, the Spireas look more like wildflowers than shrubs. Their thin stems, only two to three feet tall, are topped with clusters of small blossoms in summer. They grow alongside many of our common wildflowers, such as Milkweed, Queen Anne's Lace, and Loosestrife, and when winter comes, all remain standing with attractive dried flowerheads. But if you went to collect these plants for an arrangement of "winter weeds," you would notice one significant difference in Spirea. While the stems of the wildflowers have all died, leaving only live roots to start next year's growth, the stem of Spirea remains alive, as you can tell by scraping the bark and seeing green beneath. This is an important distinction between woody and non-woody plants; woody plants, which include shrubs, trees, and some vines, have stems that live for two or more years.

One winter, as I examined a few Spirea that were sticking up through the snow, I noticed that although their main stems were alive, the dried flowerheads at their tips were dead. I wondered how the plant would continue its growth next year. Would the flowerheads drop off? Where would new stems grow? The following spring, I returned to the Spirea and got my answer. The living buds just beneath the dead flowerhead were growing into new branches. The weight of these branches was making the original stem bend to a horizontal position, with its old flowerhead still at its tip. On older plants I found that this process repeated for several years, creating a jumble of horizontal stems with dead flowerheads at their tips, and young vertical branches growing from them. Within these masses of

§ 78 §

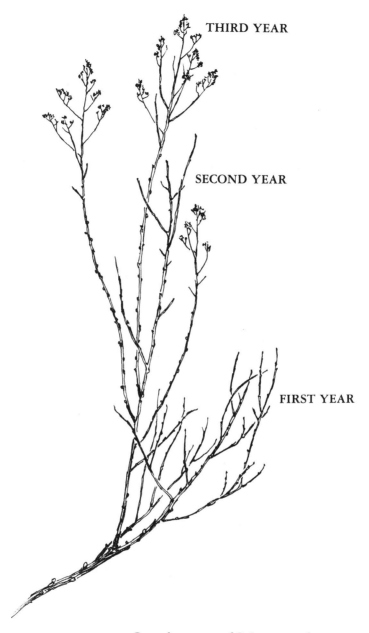

THIRD YEAR

SECOND YEAR

FIRST YEAR

Growth pattern of Spirea over three years

Spirea Cabbage Gall
and winter fruits

branches I often find Sparrows' nests and also, for some reason, a fair
number of the paper nests of White-faced Hornets.

The beautiful seed cases of Spirea stay attached to the plant throughout
the winter, and are well worth a close look. Botanists classify Spirea fruits
in the same category as the pods of Milkweeds. Both are defined as follicles
—that is, their seeds are contained in a dry casing that opens by splitting
down one side. Looking closely at the flowerhead, you will see that each
flower produces a cluster of four to five follicles. Once the follicles split
open, the seeds are shaken loose by the wind.

On the winter weed you will also discover Spirea's main insect gall, the
Spirea Cabbage Gall, formed by a small fly, *Contarinia spiraeina.* Resembling a spiny mass of plant matter, the gall always forms at the top of the

stem, stopping its further growth. Another gall, which can be seen on the leaves of the plant in summer, has been called the Spirea Pod Gall: a swelling of the leaf along the midrib makes it look like a short, stout pod. This disfiguration is also caused by a fly, *Rhabdophaga salicifolia.* Both gall-makers belong to the fly family *Cecidomyiidae,* or Gall Midges.

There are four common native species of Spirea in the East. Three of them—Meadowsweet, Broad-leaved Meadowsweet, and Corymbed Spirea —usually have white flowers in either a flat or a cone-shaped cluster. The

Meadowsweet:
left, Spirea Pod Galls on the leaves;
right, blossoms

name Meadowsweet is given to these plants collectively because of the pleasant sweet smell of their blossoms and their habit of growing in moist, sunny places, especially old meadows. On the midsummer blooms of these species you have a good chance of finding some of our larger and more spectacular beetles. One such group is the Cerambycids, or Long-horned Beetles, so named because of their long, thickened antennae, which usually curve back on either side of their body. As larvae, the beetles feed and tunnel in wood, but as adults they spend the majority of their time feeding at flowers and looking for mates. Spirea is one of their favorite haunts.

The fourth species of Spirea, Hardhack or Steeplebush, is quite different in appearance from the others. It has a thin spike of bright magenta flowers shaped like the spire of a church steeple. The name "hardhack" refers to the difficulty early farmers had with cutting them in meadows. The plants were very persistent too, for even after they were cut, they could send up new stems from their spreading roots.

Hardhack flowers are interesting for a number of reasons. First, blooming starts at the top of the spire and continues downward. Second, because its pistils (female) mature before the stamens (male) with the pollen, each bloom goes through two separate sexual stages. Therefore, when a spire of Hardhack is in bloom, the lowest flowers on the spire, those that have just opened, are female, while the older flowers, farther up the spire, are male.

What is especially intriguing about Hardhack's blooming pattern is that most other plants have flowers arranged on a spike blossom in just the opposite manner—their flowers bloom from the bottom, and each bloom is first male and then becomes female. But strangely, the final result for both types of plants is the same: the lowest flowers are female and the highest flowers are male. Does this characteristic configuration occur for a reason, or is it just a coincidence?

If you watch bees gather pollen or nectar from flowers arranged on a spike, you will notice that they tend to land at the bottom of the spike and move upward. After reaching the top, they fly to the bottom of the next spike of flowers. The bees' typical flight routine means that when they leave the top of the spike, they have just been on male flowers and are leaving with pollen; when they alight on the next spike, they land on the female

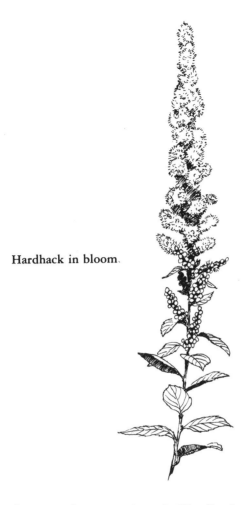

Hardhack in bloom.

flowers at the bottom. So even though Hardhack seems to bloom the opposite way from other flowers on spikes, the resulting pollination strategy is also clearly designed to optimize the chances of cross-pollination.

Of all the species in the genus *Spiraea*, Hardhack is my favorite. In early summer, the plant is inconspicuous, but later in the season, its long spires of magenta blossoms stand out in the meadows like church spires in a New England landscape, golden down covers its unbranched stems, and finely cut serrations rim its leaves. It looks as if it belonged in a formal English garden, yet here it is, lending an air of elegance to an overgrown field.

§ 83 §

CHOKEBERRY

Pyrus

ORDER: *Rosales.* FAMILY: *Rosaceae.* GENUS: *Pyrus.*
SPECIES: *P. arbutifolia,* Red Chokeberry;
P. floribunda, Purple Chokeberry; *P. melanocarpa,* Black Chokeberry.

IT IS DIFFICULT to determine why Chokeberry got a reputation so bad as to account for its common name. Whenever I have tasted its fruits, they have been pleasant and juicy, though I would also be the first to admit that there are better-tasting berries in the woods. It may be that the people who first sampled these fruits confused them with other, less agreeable ones, for Chokeberry is not all that distinctive. I find I always have to look twice before identifying the plant with confidence. Its name is easily confused with Chokecherry, which has a similar blooming time and flowers, and its fruits and leaves are much like those of Shadbush.

Chokeberry, along with Ninebark, Spirea, Chokecherry, and Shadbush, is in the Rose family. The flowers of these shrubs are similar: all have five sepals, five white petals, a large number of stamens, and three to five styles. In Chokeberry, the styles are united at their base but separate at their tips. The flowers are borne at the ends of twigs and open after the leaves have emerged. Their light color contrasts beautifully with the dark upper surface of the leaves. Since Shadbush, Chokecherry, and Chokeberry all bloom in early spring, it is fun to learn to tell them apart. Shadbush blooms earliest, and its flowers open before its leaves are fully expanded. Chokecherry tends to come next. Its flowers are on long racemes, and bloom before the leaves emerge. Chokeberry is the last of the three to bloom; its flowers, which appear after the leaves expand, are arranged in terminal umbel-like clusters.

Although the leaves of Chokeberries vary markedly from plant to plant, they are always finely toothed and dark green. Again, the leaves are similar

Chokeberry flowers

to those of Shadbush and Chokecherry and would be hard to identify positively were it not for one distinctive trait. If you look closely at the midrib on the upper surface of the Chokeberry leaf, you will see that it is covered with tiny, black, hairlike glands. You have to look carefully, but if you are lucky enough to see them, you can be certain of your identification. The function of these glands has not been determined.

Along with Chokeberry, Pears, Apples, and Mountain Ashes are also in the genus *Pyrus.* At various times in the history of botany, these four groups of plants have been classified as separate genera, but presently they are all subgenera of *Pyrus.* Chokeberry belongs to the subgenus *Aronia,* and there is still some question as to how many species *Aronia* should actually contain. The two main species, Red Chokeberry and Black Chokeberry, are most easily distinguished by the color of their fruits, respectively red and black. When fruits are not present, examine the leaf undersides and twigs of the plant: those of Red Chokeberry are most often covered with minute hairs, while those of Black Chokeberry tend to be smooth. One other pleasant difference is that the leaves of Red Chokeberry turn bright red in early fall or late summer, while those of Black Chokeberry just turn brown.

Red and Black Chokeberry have similar ranges, extending up and down

§ 85 §

Fruits of Chokeberry

the eastern half of the continent, and when growing near each other they will hybridize freely. This happens regularly, and the resulting plant is such a perfect mixture of traits that it is often considered a separate species— Purple Chokeberry. Its fruit is a color midway between red and black, and its leaves and twigs are only slightly hairy. In addition to this "pure" mixture, an entire graduation of variations between Red and Black Chokeberry is continually being discovered. It is interesting to speculate whether the two species will remain distinct in the future or finally blend into a single type.

The fruits of the two main Chokeberry species are about the size of Blueberries, but they are less sweet and far more chewy. Those of Red Chokeberry mature late in the year and remain bright red and attached to the plant during the winter. The fruits of Black Chokeberry ripen earlier in the summer and may dry and wither while still on the tips of the twigs. Birds and other animals seem to ignore the fruits of Chokeberries, which frequently go uneaten throughout the winter.

The Chokeberries often grow in wet, acidic habitats, such as the edges of bogs or swamps. In these areas, they spread rapidly and are usually found in small colonies. Their main vegetative means of reproduction is through underground roots that send up new aerial shoots. Black Chokeberry is

CHOKEBERRY

found in slightly drier habitats as well, where it tends to grow as a single plant.

The more I take the time to search out this plant and distinguish it from others, the more I discover its distinct personality. There are certain stages of yearly cycle that I particularly look forward to: in spring, the dark-red tips of its stamens form a nice design against the white petals; in summer, I enjoy the delicately tooled edges of its rich, dark-green leaves; finally, in fall, I look for the black or bright-red berries on the branches and reach out to taste one or two of them in a sort of quiet greeting to the plant.

Chokeberry winter leaf buds

SHADBUSH

Amelanchier

ORDER: *Rosales.*   FAMILY: *Rosaceae.*   GENUS: *Amelanchier.*
SPECIES: *A. arborea,* Common Shadbush, and many others.

SHADBUSH IS the earliest of our white-flowered shrubs to bloom, its flowers often opening before the leaves have fully expanded. The blossoms are composed of five thin white petals that spread out to a diameter of one to two inches. They are arranged in loose or tight racemes that are either erect or drooping, depending on the species. Once, during early spring in the Appalachian Mountains, I came across a Shadbush that was about thirty feet tall. The tips of its branches had lovely loose clusters of blossoms, and since some of the flowers were past their prime, many of the plant's petals were drifting down through the air like a late spring snow. Fluttering about the flowers were twenty or thirty Spring Azure butterflies, their wings a violet so pale that at times it was hard to distinguish them from the falling petals.

Soon after Shadbush's flowers emerge, its leaves become visible. In most eastern species, they are folded in half along their midvein while in the winter bud, and remain in this form for quite a while even after emerging. Often reddish at first, they are sometimes covered with silvery hairs on their undersides. When they are fully opened, the leaves are finely toothed. As they mature, the foliage of some species develops a deep blue-green color that is distinctive among our native shrubs.

Shadbush fruits mature by midsummer. Although they vary in quality, they generally taste good and can be collected in great quantities from the plants. Sweet, juicy fruits as large as one-half inch in diameter have been reported. At various times in history, they have been sold commercially, but for the most part they remain a marvelous wild food that goes unnoticed by humans. I have never been able to resist eating the berries right

Shadbush flowers

off the bush, but friends who have actually saved some and cooked them say that the large seeds impart a nice almond flavor to the cooked fruits. They can also be baked in pies and muffins in summer, or canned or dried for fall and winter use. The Cree Indians of Canada mixed the dried berries with pounded, dried meat and some grease to form a small, long-lasting cake of food called pemmican, which could be carried on trips.

Because they ripen so early, Shadbush berries are also utilized to a great

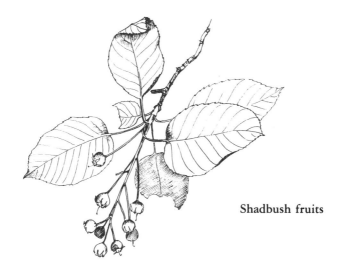

Shadbush fruits

SHADBUSH

extent by wildlife. The plant is not particularly important in comparison with other fruit-producing shrubs in eastern North America, but at least twenty-two species of birds eat the fruits and eleven species of mammals either eat the fruits or browse the twigs and foliage.

Shadbushes are most commonly seen as shrubs, but many species can reach tree height. Some species typically grow many stems from the same spot; others may also grow underground stems, which send up new aerial shoots nearby; some are often found as lone plants. I usually recognize Shadbush in winter by the color of its bark, its size, and its branching pattern. If these characteristics are inconclusive, then I look closely at the plant's buds and recent growth of twigs. The buds are long and pointed and are generally divided into both red and green portions. Sometimes you can see minute silvery hairs around their edges. The newest twigs are red-

Shadbush in winter

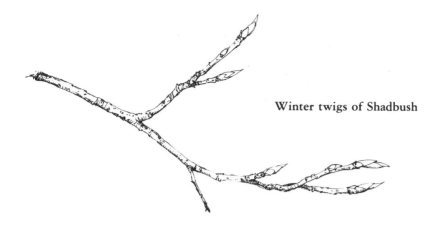

Winter twigs of Shadbush

brown, and are often covered with a whitish film that flakes off as you scrape it.

Although there are many species of *Amelanchier*, there is much disagreement on how many the genus should actually contain. The variations between plants are often slight and in some cases are thought to be the outcome of hybridization. In the last hundred years, several people have tried to sort out the different species, and each used his own system of naming them. Determining now which plants are in fact the same species but given different names in the various systems is extremely difficult. Adding to the confusion is the fact that some of the systems of classifications were established from specimens in European plant collections, and a few of these species can no longer be found growing wild in North America. In the resulting chaos, you can try to distinguish the species, if this is where your interest lies; otherwise, feel comfortably justified in forgetting the species and enjoying the natural history of the genus as a whole.

Many common names have been given to the genus *Amelanchier*, each of which is associated with an important feature of the shrub. Shadbush, one of the most common, was given to the plant by early settlers on the Atlantic seacoast. They knew that each year the Shad would leave the ocean and swim inland up clear streams to mate and lay their eggs. This migration occurred in late March to early May, and *Amelanchier*'s blooming at about the same time was a good reminder that the fish were on their spring run and could provide some fine meals. The settlers were clearly not as interested in the plant as they were in the fish, for they named Trailing Arbutus "Shadflower" for the same reason. Some species of frogs were even called Shadfrogs, for the onset of their mating calls marked the presence of the fish in the streams. The name Shadblow is also used for *Amelanchier,* "blow" being an archaic word meaning "a show of blossoms."

Amelanchier can also be found growing quite far inland, where people would of course have no reason to associate it with Shad. What was significant to them about the plant was its prolific production of fruits, a fact reflected in their names for the shrub. One of these was Juneberry, obviously referring to the fact that the fruits mature in June in some of the early-flowering species. Another name, still used in Canada, is Saskatoon. This was given to the plants and their fruits by the Blackfoot Indians, and has since also become the name of a Canadian city. Still another name that refers to the fruits is Serviceberry. This is actually a corruption of the Middle English word "serves," which in turn derived from the Latin *sorbus,* a name given to a European tree with fruits similar to those of *Amelanchier.*

In the wild, Shadbushes are generally found in the forest understory, particularly along the edges of woods or streams. The streams along which they grow on the East Coast have been greatly harmed by human activity, and many of them are seriously polluted. Even slight amounts of pollutants affect the Shad immediately, and as a result, they no longer spawn in many of these waterways. Shadbushes still produce their beautiful early blooms here, but their flowering no longer marks the run of the fishes. Let's hope that someday we will have returned the streams to their previous quality so that the name Shadbush can once again have its original meaning.

BRAMBLES

Rubus

ORDER: *Rosales.*   FAMILY: *Rosaceae.*   GENUS: *Rubus.*
SPECIES: *R. odoratus,* Purple-flowering Raspberry;
R. parviflorus, Thimbleberry; *R. phoenicolasius,* Wineberry;
R. idaeus, Raspberry; *R. occidentalis,* Black Raspberry;
R. allegheniensis, Blackberry, and many others.

I ALWAYS USED to think of the Brambles as strictly sunny-area plants, growing along the edges of fields, roads, or old paths. But in fact, Dewberries are often found growing in thin-canopied forests, and in the south, certain species of Blackberries typically grow in the understory of old woods, accompanied by other shade-tolerant plants, such as Wild Hydrangea, Highbush Blueberry, and Viburnum.

One could easily argue that many of the Brambles, such as the Blackberries and Raspberries, are not actually woody plants at all. They never have a true bark, and although their roots are often perennial, their stems are biennial, that is, they have a life cycle of only two years. The first year, the root system produces long unbranched canes, which grow leaves but no flowers. The second year, these same canes grow smaller side branches, which produce flowers that later mature into fruits. After producing fruits, the canes die back, but the roots remain living and send up new shoots the following year.

The flowers of Brambles are loose and delicate, and their petals are shed soon after the blossoms open. Once the petals fall, you will notice that the anthers wither and drop over the edges of the calyx. At this point, there is in the center of the flower a miniature green version of the familiar fruit, composed of many tiny separate sections. If you look closely at these parts, you will see that each has a small projecting hair, which is actually the former pistil of the flower. This small fruit gradually enlarges and finally it changes from green to dark red or black. If you pull this ripened berry

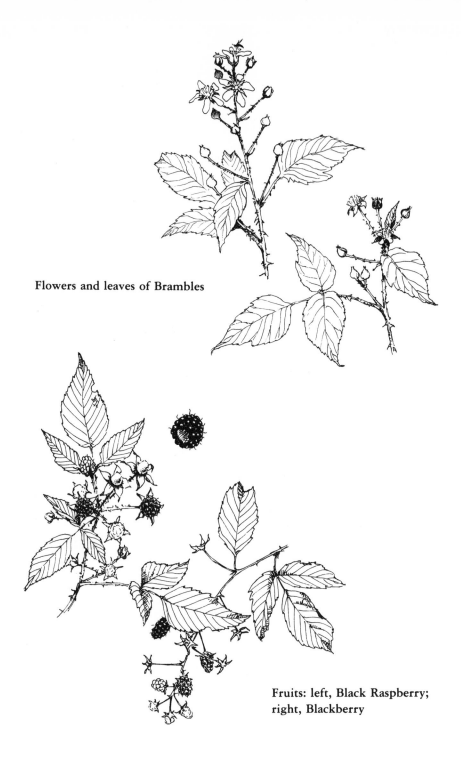

Flowers and leaves of Brambles

Fruits: left, Black Raspberry;
right, Blackberry

BRAMBLES

off a Raspberry plant, a small spongy cone is left at the tip of the stem. This cone is the original flower's receptacle, on which were attached numerous carpels, each developing into a separate part of the fruit.

Raspberries detach easily from their receptacle, giving the picked fruits the appearance of small cups. This is not the case with the fruits of Blackberries and Dewberries; because they remain attached to their receptacles, they are harder to pluck off, and have no indentation once picked. Even if undisturbed, the fruits of Raspberry will fall to the ground once they are ripe; those of Dewberry and Blackberry, however, will often dry on the plant. I have often wondered why these two different patterns have developed within the same genus and what advantages exist in each strategy.

The fruits of Brambles are technically not berries, but aggregations of small drupes. Though this distinction may seem merely semantic, it actually affects you every time you eat the fruits. The seeds of drupes have especially hard coatings, and in the case of the Brambles, they often resist being crushed as you chew, and end up lodged between your teeth. I find this to be especially true of Blackberries.

Brambles produce more food for wildlife than any other shrub in eastern North America. Not only are the fruits eaten, but the leaves and stems are grazed as well. Over a hundred birds and mammals are known to feed on this genus. But nutrition is not its only value. Since most Brambles spread by underground roots that send up a large number of new shoots, the plants often form dense groves—superb cover for the various homes and activities of animals. You might guess that many birds would nest in this foliage, but in my experience, this has not proved to be the case. Despite its density,

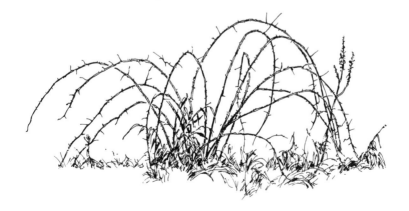

Branches of Black Raspberry rooting at their tips

BRAMBLES

the branching pattern of Brambles may not form suitable supports for nests. Birds that do nest among the plants generally use the ground beneath them.

The genus *Rubus* contains over two hundred species divided into five subgenera, three of which have members that are shrubs. The subgenus *Anaplobatus* contains two shrubs, Thimbleberry and Purple-flowering Raspberry. These species differ from all other Brambles in that they have no thorns, their leaves are simple, with lobes resembling those of Maple, and their flowers have broad, spreading petals. Purple-flowering Raspberry is also our only common species of Bramble that does not have white flowers.

The subgenus *Idaeobatus* contains only three shrub species, the plants we commonly know as Raspberries. They are distinguished from *Anaplobatus* by their prickly stems, compound leaves, and small petals. Wineberry has a stem covered with dense, soft, red bristles. Red Raspberry has sparse prickles and branches that do not root at their tips. Black Raspberry also has sparse prickles, but typically roots at its branch tips.

My first introduction to Wineberries was through an aunt who made a beautifully colored jelly from the fruits and always served it with toast in

Stems of Brambles:
left, Blackberry;
right, Black Raspberry

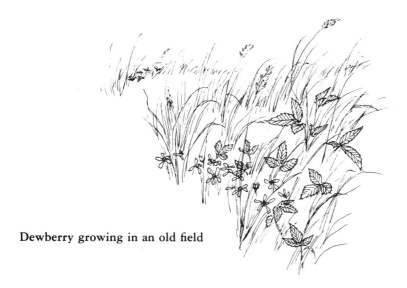

Dewberry growing in an old field

the morning when I visited her. It is my favorite wild jelly, and its flavor is etched into my taste buds in such a way that I will never forget it. Where I live now, Red Raspberries and Black Raspberries are more common. I prefer the latter, and I am always on the lookout for its light purple, arching stems, which root at their tips.

The third subgenus, *Eubatus,* is far larger than the others and contains almost two hundred species. Included in these are the Dewberries and the Blackberries. The former are generally low trailing vines; the latter are always arching canes, distinguished from other Brambles by their five-sided, fluted stems. These plants hybridize freely, and there is much disagreement on the number of species that should be recognized.

The most enjoyable moments that I have had with Brambles have always been while eating the fruits. Sometimes particular plants remain in my memory, such as the one my wife and I discovered while on a canoe trip in the lakes of northern Maine. We had been paddling all morning and stopped at a point where an old dirt road met the edge of the lake. As we got out of the canoe, we spotted across the road a plant loaded down with red jewels. It was a wild Red Raspberry bush and its fruits were large and soft and fell off into our cupped hands at the slightest touch. They were gently warmed by the midday sun and were sweeter than any I have ever tasted since.

ROSE

Rosa

ORDER: *Rosales.*   FAMILY: *Rosaceae.*   GENUS: *Rosa.*
SPECIES: *R. setigera,* Prairie Rose;
R. multiflora, Multiflora Rose; *R. nitida,* Shining Rose;
R. virginiana, Virginia Rose; *R. palustris,* Swamp Rose;
R. carolina, Pasture Rose; *R. rugosa,* Rugosa Rose;
R. blanda, Smooth Rose, and many others.

ROSES ARE SO OFTEN associated with florist shops and cultivated gardens that we tend to forget or overlook the beautiful wild Roses that grow naturally in our woods and fields. Cultivated Roses are all specially bred to have many rows of petals to please our sense of form. Wild Roses, however, are not designed to charm us but to attract pollinators. For this purpose, they find that a single row of five petals works superbly.

Rose flowers have a very simple pollination strategy. The pistils are all arranged in the center of the flower, surrounded by a ring of stamens. Although the stigmas and the anthers mature simultaneously, self-pollination is avoided to some degree by the fact that the stamens bend away from the center of the flower. Bumblebees, which are one of the roses' main pollinators, collect nectar from the nectiferous ring at the base of the stamens, and then gather pollen. Because of their tendency to land in the center of the flower, they often first come in contact with the receptive stigmas and thus cause some cross-pollination.

The rose's sepals, petals, and anthers are all attached to the top of the floral cup, a container in which the seeds develop. As the seeds (actually achenes) mature, the cup expands into a fleshy covering, which we commonly call the hip. The hip becomes very thick and juicy in a few species of Roses, remaining rather thin and hard in others. In some species, the five

Bumblebee on a flower
of Pasture Rose

sepals remain attached to the top of the floral cup, even after the seeds have matured, and in this position they always remind me of the collar of a court jester. Other species shed the sepals and the final fruit has a fairly smooth top.

One of our most productive species of Rose in terms of fruit output is Multiflora Rose, a plant introduced from Japan but rapidly becoming widespread up and down the East Coast. From my observation, very few of its fruits are eaten by migrating birds in fall; in winter, they are eaten primarily

Matured Rose hips

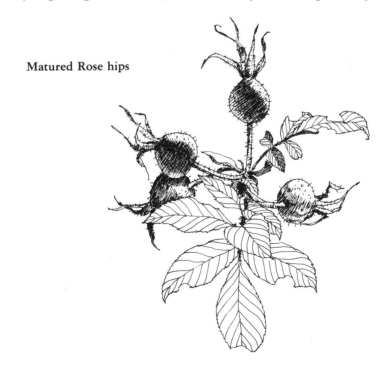

by Robins and Mockingbirds. One commonly sees little mounds of chewed-apart fruits beneath the bushes, or filling old birds' nests built in the plants. For many years these piles, especially those in the birds' nests, were a mystery to me. Who had begun to feed on the fruits? Why were they left in birds' nests? Why were both the pulp and the seeds uneaten?

These questions were partially answered when I went out walking with another naturalist, who examined the fruits more closely than I had done. She pointed out that although the hips had not been eaten, the seeds had been removed and each one gnawed, so that only its hard outer shell remained. We guessed that this was the work of a mouse that crawled out to the fruiting branches, collected a few fruits in its mouth, and then went back to a central place to take them apart and eat the centers. Apparently, the abandoned birds' nests made a perfect spot for eating, but when none were available the mouse used particular spots on the ground. We had a marvelous time using our eyes and minds to learn something new directly from nature. I find this process one of the greatest joys of being a naturalist, and it is a joy accessible to anyone who has the desire to learn and the patience to make careful observations.

In late winter and early spring, you can often see other evidence of feeding on rosebushes. Examine the base of the stems, and you have a good

Mockingbird nest
in Multiflora Rose

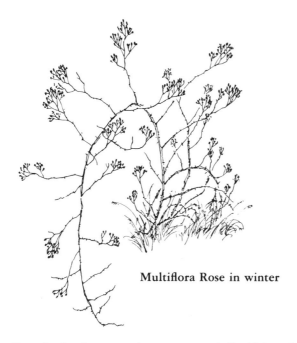

Multiflora Rose in winter

chance of finding the bark gnawed away, especially if the plants are growing near old fields. This is the work of the Meadow Vole, a rodent that apparently prefers this bark over that of most other plants. You will also see its tunnels radiating out from the base of the plant, through the grass or snow. Where tunnels meet, there are often piles of its droppings, which it seems to leave in carefully selected areas. Other animals that feed on the plants include Pheasants, which eat the fruits, and Rabbits, which nibble the shoots and also gnaw the bark.

Of course, we use Roses for food as well. In his book *Stalking the Healthful Herbs,* Euell Gibbons has a marvelous chapter called "How to Eat a Rose." He describes how easy it is to make uncooked Rose petal jam and a small still in which you can brew Rose water, and also shares a recipe for Rose hip fruit soup. Of course, Rose hips can also be eaten right off the bush. The best species for this foraging is the introduced species, Rugosa Rose, which grows along beaches on the eastern seaboard. It has the largest fruits, some growing to nearly an inch in diameter. Eat them just after they have turned red and become soft, for they are juiciest at this point. Later in the season, they become dry inside and contain hairlike filaments around the seeds. As is now widely known, Rose hips, for comparable weights, contain about one hundred times as much vitamin C as do oranges.

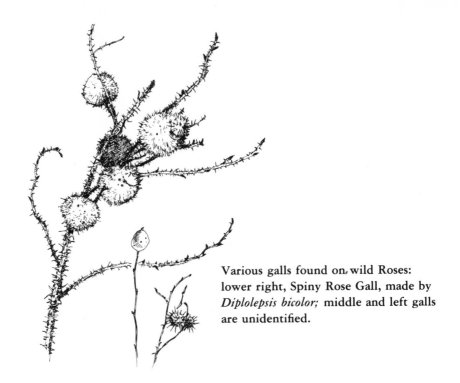

Various galls found on wild Roses:
lower right, Spiny Rose Gall, made by
Diplolepis bicolor; middle and left galls
are unidentified.

Because it forms dense thickets and its leaves emerge early in the season, Multiflora Rose is a superb nesting site for birds. The nests that I find most frequently among its arching branches are those of Mockingbirds, Catbirds, Brown Thrashers, Yellow Warblers, and Song Sparrows. Except for the nest of the Yellow Warbler, which tends to deteriorate during the summer, the nests of these species are quickly spotted in winter, when the plant has shed its leaves. Deer Mice frequently convert the nests into winter homes. These adapted structures can be easily recognized, for they no longer have a depression in the center, but are piled high with grasses and other downy plant material. If you decide to open one up, do it gently, for you have a good chance of finding a mouse inside.

Whenever you come across a wild Rose, take a moment to search for galls, since Roses, like Willows and Oaks, are utilized by many gall insects.

ROSE

Most of the fifty or more varieties of gall found on Roses are caused by small wasps that belong to the genus *Diplolepsis,* in the family *Cynipidae.* Some of these have remarkably beautiful shapes, such as the Spiny Rose Gall, made by *Diplolepsis bicolor.* It is a small sphere with delicate spines projecting in all directions. The Mossy Rose Gall looks like a bunch of moss the size of a golf ball growing on the twig; it is made by *D. rosae.* A third common gall, formed by *D. globuloides,* appears on the twigs as a small potato-like growth. I find that the majority of galls are found on our truly native species; introduced species, such as Multiflora Rose and Rugosa Rose, tend to be less afflicted.

If you find that you have trouble distinguishing one species of native Rose from another, or that their characteristics never quite match those in the identification guide, do not despair: it is the fault of neither you nor the guides. The fact is that where our native species overlap in range, they

Leaves and stipules
of Multiflora Rose

frequently hybridize. Additionally, there is really no one characteristic that you can use to tell one native species from another. You usually have to use a number of qualities, such as growth habit, presence or absence of spines on certain parts, the shape of the stipules, and the quality and shapes of the leaves, to determine a species accurately. For greatly simplified categories, you can divide the genus into the climbing or trailing Roses, which include Multiflora Rose and Prairie Rose, and the upright shrubs, which include Smooth Rose, Swamp Rose, Pasture Rose, Rugosa Rose, Shining Rose, and Virginia Rose. Of the latter group, only Rugosa Rose and Shining Rose have dense bristles along their upper branches; the others have scattered thorns or none at all.

In my study I have a tiny chest of drawers made from old cigar boxes, which belonged to my grandfather. In many of the drawers I have put some of my favorite scents from the natural world. One box holds some Wild Honey Comb, another a few leaves from Sage gathered in the prairies of the Midwest, a third has Rose petals that I collected one summer. Now dried, they still smell marvelous. Occasionally I open the Rose petal drawer and find that, with each year, the perfume from the petals seems to get richer and deeper. I am not sure why, but when I try to describe the smell, the term "old-fashioned" comes to mind.

Multiflora Rose in an old meadow

CHERRY, PLUM

Prunus

ORDER: *Rosales.*   FAMILY: *Rosaceae.*   GENUS: *Prunus.*
SPECIES: *P. maritima,* Beach Plum; *P. americana,* Wild Plum;
P. virginiana, Chokecherry, and many others.

ALL OUR CHERRIES and Plums belong to the genus *Prunus.* Although most
are tree-size, a few typically remain small and so are considered to be
shrubs. A characteristic that all members of the genus share and one that
is a foolproof identification at any time of year is the special odor that is
released when the bark of their young twigs is scraped. To me, the scent
falls somewhere between strong cherry cough syrup and stale cigars. The
most potent odor seems to come from the Chokecherry, rather than from
any of the Plums. Another interesting way to identify members of this
genus in any season is to look for a common and obvious deformation of
their twigs and branches. This condition, called Black Knot, is caused by
a fungus, *Plowrightia morbosa,* and appears as black, irregular swellings on
the twigs and branches. With age, the swellings crack and fissure and often
produce a gelatinous material. A number of insects have adapted to breeding within the shelter of these deformations, which led early naturalists to
suspect mistakenly that Black Knot was caused by the insects themselves.

Susceptibility to attack by Tent Caterpillars is another common characteristic of this genus. In summer, the adult moth lays its eggs in a shiny mass
that forms a small collar around new twigs. The eggs do not hatch until the
following spring, almost nine months later. Once hatched, the caterpillars
make in the crotches of branches familiar tentlike web nests. The caterpillars leave the nest only for brief periods, to feed on leaves. Once the larvae
are mature, they abandon the nest and make cocoons in protected places.
These cocoons are often found in early summer and are quite distinctive:
white and about an inch long, they give off a chalky dust when flicked

Old Tent Caterpillar nest and egg case

Black Knot on Cherry twig

slightly. The adult moths emerge in midsummer and soon mate and lay their eggs. The egg cases are very easy to identify and if you want to protect a particular plant from the caterpillars in the coming spring, just break off any egg cases you find during the previous winter.

One April, I discovered a feature of Chokecherry flowers that I had never expected to find. It was a day of mixed sensations, for in the winter landscape the air and the sun's warmth felt like spring. In an open field I came across a small group of Chokecherries in bloom. As I approached, I realized that myriads of insects were attracted to the flowers. At first, this seemed strange, since I had encountered so few insects elsewhere. But as I thought about it, I realized that the air was warm enough for the insects to be active, and since there were as yet very few flowers for them to feed on, they would naturally gather in great numbers on the earliest blooms.

I took out my notebook, sat down in the warm sunlight, and started to draw the different types of insects that were attending the flowers. Two delicate butterflies were sipping nectar. One was the Spring Azure, a small violet butterfly that is one of the first to emerge in spring. The other, a close

Chokecherry flowers
with butterfly

relative, but coppery brown, was so unconcerned with my presence that I could practically pick it up in my hand. There were also many types of flies: one large iridescent one that shone red and green in the sunlight; other, smaller flies, colored like bees, which hovered in midair about the plant; and a dark fly that chose the white pages of my journal as a perch as soon as I opened it. Of course, I saw many bees as well—Bumblebees of various sizes, Honeybees, and probably some solitary bees. Finally, crawling along the stems and over the flowers were hordes of ants.

Beside the insects at the flowers, there were also a few Tent Caterpillar nests. One Chokecherry had already been completely defoliated of its emerging leaves, and the caterpillar nest in its branches held many dead larvae. I began to wonder what happens to Tent Caterpillars that have eaten themselves out of house and home. Their witnessed fate seemed the most likely one, since they had settled on a Chokecherry, a small plant with very few leaves. Would the insects now migrate to new sources of food, or would they just die off? The answers will take further observation.

The fruits of Cherries and Plums are called drupes—that is, their seed

Chokecherry fruits

is contained in a hardened coating that is in turn surrounded by fleshy material. The seed with its hardened exterior is called the pit, and as you can probably recall from eating Cherries or Plums, the pits of these fruits each have a different shape. The Cherry pit is basically round, while that of the Plum is larger and somewhat flattened, with a slight ridge where the flattened sides come together. It is difficult to say what purpose the different shapes serve, but it is clear from wildlife studies that the two fruits have a greatly variable appeal to animals.

After Oaks, Pines, and Blackberries, the Cherry is our most important woody wildlife plant, its fruits primarily being consumed by birds, but also to some extent by Bears, Foxes, Raccoons, Chipmunks, and Mice. Plums are not known to be eaten in any considerable quantity by birds, but are eaten a fair amount by Foxes. It may be that within the genus *Prunus,* Cherries have evolved to be dispersed primarily by birds, while the Plum has evolved to be dispersed by mammals. Birds can certainly eat an entire Cherry and void its pit, but would not be able to do the same with a Plum.

The best variety of Plums for human consumption is the Beach Plum, which grows along most of the eastern coast. Although the inland American Plum is especially sweet in some localities, its flavor varies widely. Among the Cherries, the Chokecherry is the only edible shrub variety, and despite its name, I find its ripe fruits a refreshing treat. However, try to avoid swallowing the pits, which contain cyanide.

Even if you don't eat the fruits of Chokecherries, it is worth seeking them out for their beauty. They are shiny, translucent, and bright red, and with the afternoon sun behind them they literally light up. The loveliness of the Chokecherry is similar to that of the mature fruits of False Solomon's Seal, which can be found in late fall. If you have not yet experienced the brilliant color of either of these fruits, then make a point of seeing them in the coming year.

BRISTLY LOCUST

Robinia

ORDER: *Rosales.*   FAMILY: *Leguminosae.*   GENUS: *Robinia.*
SPECIES: *R. hispida,* Bristly Locust.

IF YOU VISIT Bristly Locust in fall or winter, you will immediately know why it is called bristly. With the leaves gone, the lovely, reddish-golden bristles that cover most of the plant are easily seen. In fall, the seed pods can also be found hanging on the plants; their bristles are short and extremely dense. If you hold a pod in your hand and rub your fingers across it, it creates a pleasant sound, similar to that made when you run your thumb over the teeth of a fine-toothed comb. The softer bristles that line the branches are most prominent on the newer growth, having worn off the older stems. I was once near a group of these plants late in the afternoon of a bright fall day. The sun, low on the horizon and behind the plants, illuminated all the bristles on the upper twigs, making their fine branching glow. I have enjoyed a similar sight in winter with the velvety twigs of Staghorn Sumac.

On this same fall day, I realized that while in many cases the leaflets from the compound leaves had been shed from the petioles, the petioles themselves remained attached to the plant. They were now dried and curved, and formed practically complete circles, adding greatly to the linear beauty of the winter plant. As I touched one of the petioles, it broke off in my hand, but where it had been attached to the twig, a beautiful amber spot now shone in the light. It was the leaf bud, covered with golden silky hairs. Though the bud was small, when held directly in the light it looked more like real gold than anything else I know of in the plant kingdom. It was certainly an unexpected treat.

Bristly Locust can be found growing along roads or the edges of fields in fine, dry soil. Since this species has a spreading root system that continu-

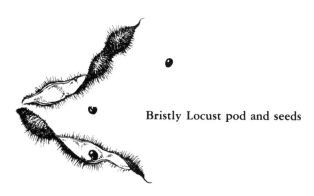

Bristly Locust pod and seeds

ally sends up new aerial stems, a number of plants usually grow in the same area. Like many other legumes, the plant has the ability to fix atmospheric nitrogen through certain bacteria on its roots, and therefore tends to enrich any soil in which it grows.

The leaves of Bristly Locust are pinnately compound and similar to those of Black Locust, except that each of its leaflets is tipped by a small bristle which is a continuation of the midvein. The flower buds emerge soon after the leaves have expanded and start to open in early summer. They are a shocking pink and hang off the plant in luxuriant, drooping clusters. New

Bristly Locust twigs and
leaf petiole in winter

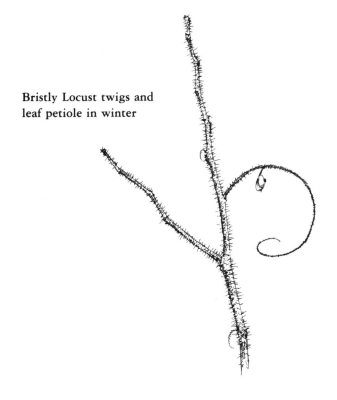

Bristly Locust leaves and flowers

flowers may continue to open through much of the summer, but the main blooming period is May and June. Black Locust, a closely related plant, is well known for the heady fragrance of its flowers and the myriads of bees they attract, but the flowers of Bristly Locust have little fragrance and are only occasionally visited by insects. The pollination mechanism of these flowers is similar to that of many other legumes and is described in detail in the section of this book that deals with Wisteria.

Bristly Locust actually has a very restricted natural range, limited to the mountains of Virginia and Tennessee and down into Georgia. Because of the plant's lovely pink flowers, however, it has been planted widely as an ornamental. From these settings, it has spread into the wild, so that it is now found scattered up and down the eastern half of the continent.

One of my favorite times to visit Bristly Locust is in midsummer, when two marvelous events take place on the leaves, events that occur not only on this species but also on the more common tree species, Black Locust. One of these is the appearance of light blotches on the upper surface of the

§ 112 §

leaflets. There is usually only one blotch per leaflet and each has the same form—roughly amoeboid, with short extensions radiating out from the center. If you turn a leaflet over, you will see a spot of dark material near the center of the blotch. This is the work of a tiny female moth, *Parectopa robiniella,* which laid single eggs on a number of Bristly Locust leaflets. A small, flattened caterpillar hatched from each egg, burrowed into the leaflet and started to eat the upper layer of cells just beneath its surface. The eaten-away area is called a "mine"; this particular form is called a digitate mine, since it radiates out in fingerlike projections. After the larva had eaten, it chewed a small compartment in the lower layer of the leaf, and whenever it had to defecate or shed its skin, it left the waste in this cavity, which you see as the dark spot on the underside of the leaf. The larvae leave the plant when they are fully grown, to pupate on the ground among the grasses.

Another signature left on the leaves of Locust, either the shrub or the tree, is a cut made into the midvein of the leaflets. The resulting flap is

Leaflets of Bristly Locust:
upper leaves have mines of moth,
Parectopa robiniella;
lower leaves have folds
from Silver-spotted Skipper larvae.

BRISTLY LOCUST

folded over and pleated at the edges to form a small tent, all held in place with silk. If you open one of these tents carefully, you will find inside a tiny, greenish-yellow caterpillar with a black head; its body tapers sharply to a point just behind the head. This is the caterpillar of the Silver-spotted Skipper, a common species whose adults choose the leaflets of Locusts or other legumes on which to lay their eggs. When the caterpillar grows too large to fit inside one of these tents, it ties two adjacent leaflets together with silk, leaving one end open through which it can crawl out at night to feed on other leaflets. When fully grown, it leaves the plant and makes its cocoon in a protected place near the ground. The adults emerge in June; they are about two inches across and have chocolate-brown wings with white and yellow markings. In midsummer, look for their darting flight about the Bristly Locusts, where they are seeking out with an inborn recognition the perfect place to lay their eggs.

Silver-spotted Skipper
with Locust leaves

WISTERIA

Wisteria

ORDER: *Rosales.*   FAMILY: *Leguminosae.*   GENUS: *Wisteria.*
SPECIES: *W. frutescens,* Wisteria; *W. sinensis,* Chinese Wisteria;
W. floribunda, Japanese Wisteria.

I REMEMBER VIVIDLY the long clusters of flowers hanging like bunches of grapes from the Wisteria vine on the side of my grandmother's house. Since I grew up in the north and Wisteria grows wild only farther south, my few associations with the vine were near houses, where it was generally small and attached to trellises. But recently I came upon Wisteria in its native haunt, and saw its strong stems reach up over cliffs and trees with ease and its lush blossoms cascade down from the vine's heights. This discovery has given me a new sense of the plant; instead of its being a sign of human presence, as it is in the north, it became for me more a majestic remnant of the past, providing a rare glimpse of the character of the prehuman landscape.

Like Bittersweet, Honeysuckle, Dutchman's-Pipe, and Nightshade, Wisteria climbs by twisting and twining about its supports. Its winding around the trunks of trees can definitely be damaging to the tree as both plants expand in girth, but even more harmful to the tree is the loss of light caused by the large compound leaves that are abundant on the vines. At the base of these leaves are two short appendages that look like small horns, which remain after the leaves have fallen and even for a year or two thereafter. In some cases, I have noticed that they help to hook the new growth onto the supporting plant or surface. They point slightly back along the stem and remind me of Multiflora Rose's backward-turning thorns, also used to climb over branches and up into trees.

Wisteria flowers are similar to those of many other legumes. Once you understand their pollination mechanism, you can appreciate it in all other plants with the same structure of flower, from the minute version in the Clover or the Vetches, to the more easily observed Peas and Beans of your vegetable garden. The legume flower generally has five petals, which are divided into three different types. The largest petal, called the "standard," is bent upward and acts as the main visual advertisement of the flower. Right below the standard are two vertical petals fused together along their base. They are called the "keel" and contain the anthers and a single pistil. On either side of the keel are the two remaining petals, the "wings," whose function has not been definitely established.

Bees are Wisteria's main pollinators and are first attracted by the color and odor of the bloom. As the insect arrives, it is oriented by the structure of the flower to land on the keel, where, between the base of the keel and the base of the standard, it begins to probe for nectar. To reach its food,

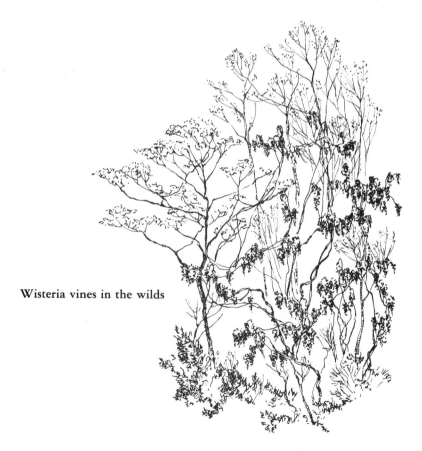

Wisteria vines in the wilds

Wisteria flowers

the bee must force its way into the flower; this action, along with the weight of the insect, pushes down on the keel. The pistil, which is stiffer than the anthers, is the first to pop up through the slit in the keel. It brushes against the underside of the insect, where it becomes covered with pollen, presumably from another Wisteria flower that the bee has previously visited. The anthers spring up immediately after the pistil and dust the insect's belly with fresh pollen, which it will then take to the next flower as it searches for more nectar.

In our native Wisterias, the flower cluster matures only a few blossoms at a time, starting at the top and progressing down to the tip. Since there are only a few flowers in bloom in each cluster, this forces the insects to move more from flower cluster to flower cluster and from plant to plant, which increases the chances for cross-pollination. Japanese and Chinese Wisterias have looser flower clusters, about twice as long as those of our native species. Like our native plants, the flowers of Japanese Wisteria bloom a few at a time on each cluster, but those of Chinese Wisteria tend to bloom almost simultaneously, suggesting that it might have a slightly different strategy for pollination.

The pods of Wisteria are as interesting as its flowers. In the introduced species, they are covered with small hairs, giving them the texture of velvet. When turned in the light, the pod refracts the sun's rays in varying ways,

Opened pods of native Wisteria

producing a shimmer of different colors. The pods of the native species are about half as long (three to five inches) and have no hairs. As is true of many other legumes, their structure is a mechanism designed to shoot the seeds into the air and away from the competition of the parent plant.

I once brought some Wisteria pods into my study and left them on my desk. That night I was awakened by an extremely sharp and loud woody shattering sound. I got up and looked around the house, and having found nothing wrong, went back to sleep. It wasn't until a few days later that the incident made sense. I was absentmindedly looking at the pods and suddenly realized that they had opened. They had split, and each half was curled into a spiral just like the horns of an African antelope. The coils were so tough that I could not unbend them. I looked around for the seeds and found one or two on the far side of the room.

If you look closely at opened Wisteria pods, you will see that they are composed of two layers. These dry at different rates—the inner layer faster

§ 118 §

than the outer one—creating a powerful tension that will suddenly split the pod open with a loud "crack" and shoot the seeds in all directions. The seeds of our native species are about the size of peas but flat, rectangular, and shiny, while those of the introduced species are flattened disks about the size of a dime.

As vines, Wisterias represent one of evolution's answers to the problem of competing for sunlight. Instead of being restricted to growing in the open, or having to produce thick stems to compete with trees, they simply climb up over existing plants, using them as a support to reach the sunlight. Once a vine like Wisteria reaches the top of a tree, it often produces such a quantity of leaves that it shades the supporting tree to death. This is part of the mixed blessing of vines: although I love to see and smell Wisteria's blooms in spring and enjoy its velvety pods in fall, I would feel differently about the vine if I found it growing up over a favorite tree.

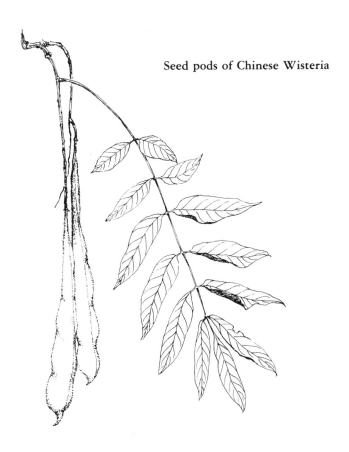

Seed pods of Chinese Wisteria

HOPTREE

Ptelea

ORDER: *Geraniales.*   FAMILY: *Rutaceae.*   GENUS: *Ptelea.*
SPECIES: *P. trifoliata,* Hoptree.

HOPTREE BELONGS to the same family as all the trees that produce our citrus fruits—*Rutaceae.* A common characteristic of this family is that all its species have pungent or bitter-aromatic leaves, fruits, and bark. There are only two genera in *Rutaceae* that are native to eastern North America: *Xanthoxylum* (Prickly Ash) and *Ptelea* (Hoptree). Hoptree is the only species of *Ptelea* in the East. With its thick trunk and widespread branching, Hoptree might be considered a tree, but because it often grows many stems from the same spot and is rarely more than fifteen feet tall, it qualifies equally as a shrub.

Wingseed, Wafer Ash, Hoptree, Quinine Tree, Shrubby Trefoil, Ptelea —these are just some of the common names *Ptelea trifoliata* has inspired, each one pointing to a different characteristic of the plant. Two of its names —Quinine Tree, and the most widely accepted common name, Hoptree— are the result of the efforts of early colonists to find uses for American plants, hoping to discover the new wonder drugs of the day. It must have been an exciting time to be a medicinal botanist. The plants of Europe had been already experimented with for hundreds of years, but in North America, new plants were everywhere, and once again one had the chance of making an important discovery. Specimens of the flora, which were often sent to Europe, fueled the expectations of experimenters. Plants that had any usual aroma or taste were the first to be suspected of having curing powers. Hoptree fit this description: its leaves were aromatic and the bark from its roots was extremely bitter. The bitterness of the root attracted the most attention and was considered to be useful as a tonic, or invigorating drink. It was also thought that it might be a substitute for quinine—thus

HOPTREE

Quinine Tree. The name Hoptree came about not because the fruits looked like hops, but because they were thought to be a possible replacement for the hops that were put into beer. Most of these promises of medicinal or economic value faded over the years.

Whatever its failures as a medicinal, Hoptree has remained a popular ornamental, valued for its pleasant form and lovely foliage. Because it has basically an untoothed compound leaf, Hoptree is slightly reminiscent of ash, hence the name Wafer Ash. There are even records of Thomas Jefferson writing from Paris to the well-known naturalist John Bartram, Jr., in Philadelphia, asking for seeds of Hoptree along with some other plants. Hoptree eventually became widespread in European gardens. Many horticultural varieties were subsequently created, some of which were then sent back to America for ornamental use.

If you scrape the bark of Hoptree's twigs, you will meet up with a strong odor that has been aptly described as similar to that of a Bobcat. In winter, twigs look practically dead, since the buds of next year's leaves are extremely small and buried in the leaf scars of the previous year. The twigs are often quite black due to the presence of the Two-spotted Treehopper, which sucks sap and leaves a residue of honeydew. See the section on Bittersweet for a complete life history of the Treehopper.

Flowers and leaves of Hoptree

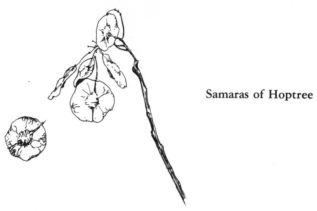

Samaras of Hoptree

The flowers of Hoptree bloom in early summer. They are greenish, are borne in clusters, and have either four or five small petals, depending on the blossom. The flowers are polygamous, which simply means that they are not very predictable—they may be only male, only female, or have characteristics of both sexes. They are inconspicuous to the eye but evident to the nose and ear. Their strong smell, which wafts downwind from the shrub, is usually described as unpleasant, but I do not find it so. It has been suggested that their odor may attract pollinating flies that are seeking carrion, but from studies of the insect visitors to the flowers, it is clear that the flies do not agree. The most common flies on the flowers are the Syrphid and Tachnid flies, and neither is particularly attracted to carrion. What makes the flowers conspicuous to the ear is the abundance of Honeybees that they attract. I love to put my head among the blossoms and be surrounded by the fragrance and the buzz of these insects.

Another of Hoptree's common names, Wingseed, comes from the form of its fruit, which begins growing in midsummer and matures and turns brown in fall. Like the fruits of Maples or Ashes, that of Hoptree is technically a samara. In this type of fruit, the seed grows in the ovary of the plant and the wall of the ovary develops into the wing. Elm seeds are also samaras and their fruits are so similar to those of Hoptree that Linnaeus gave Hoptree the Greek name for Elm, *Ptelea*. The veins of the wing have a beautiful symmetry and demonstrate a very simple and marvelous principle of distribution, for as they radiate out from the center, they neatly subdivide, like the delta of a river. At the very tip of the samara you may see a small filament, the remains of the style from the pistil.

Most samaras have been engineered to twirl as they drop. The wing or blade presses against the air as the fruit falls, effectively slowing its descent and allowing more time for the wind to blow it laterally. This mechanism functions only if the fruit drops from a point high enough off the ground. Samaras are therefore found exclusively on trees or small shrubs. Smaller herbaceous plants, such as Goldenrod or Dandelion, generally have a parachute of filaments and a light seed so that the fruit can be lifted by the wind and out of the way of interfering vegetation.

After thinking about samaras, I began to wonder how the wing of Hoptree worked. Did it just fall haphazardly, with its wing slowing the descent, or would there in fact be more order to its movement? I went outside and collected a few Hoptree seeds from a nearby field and brought them into my study to see how they fell in still air. I stood on my desk chair and dropped one from as high as I could. In the first foot of its fall it tumbled a bit, but then righted itself and remained level for the next eight feet. I tried it again, and then with other samples, and the result was always the same. Looking more closely at the samaras, I found that in each case, their edges were bent up to one side only. I dropped a few more of the fruits and found that indeed, no matter how you started one, it always righted itself with the same side up. This discovery showed me once again how wondrous the details of evolution are. What I might have first passed off as just a wing that helped the seed get caught in the wind turned out to be a finely tuned aerodynamic structure that fell horizontally through the air, always with the same side facing upward. For me, this type of glimpse into the refinement of adaptations in the living things with which I share the planet makes me far more careful in my dealings with them. It is like hearing skilled old-time folk musicians and suddenly realizing the incredible artistry that is behind their seemingly casual music.

Hoptree in winter

SUMAC

Rhus

ORDER: *Sapindales.*   FAMILY: *Anacardiaceae.*   GENUS: *Rhus.*
SPECIES: *R. typhina,* Staghorn Sumac; *R. glabra,* Smooth Sumac;
R. copallina, Dwarf Sumac; *R. aromatica,* Fragrant Sumac;
R. Vernix, Poison Sumac; *R. radicans,* Poison Ivy;
R. Toxicodendron, Poison Oak.

SO OFTEN WE FIND Sumacs in our cities, thriving in disturbed land such as that along railroad lines, in vacant lots, or in the little patches of industrial areas that have not yet been sealed over with macadam. They share these areas with many introduced species, plants that can dominate open areas but cannot survive the basic forest habitat of eastern North America. Their present distribution makes me wonder where the native Sumacs lived before humans arrived and began to clear the land.

The genus *Rhus* is generally divided into three groups. The first consists of tall, woody species that produce cones of red fruits at the tips of their branches. This group includes Dwarf Sumac, Staghorn Sumac, and Smooth Sumac. Dwarf Sumac is strangely named, for it often grows taller than any of our other species. It has finer branching and smaller compound leaves than the other members of this group. Its leaf is unique in that growing along the midrib that connects the leaflets are leafy appendages. This characteristic and the fact that the leaves are shiny explain the other common names for this species: Wing-rib Sumac and Shining Sumac.

I always enjoy differentiating between Staghorn Sumac and Smooth Sumac, since their names so clearly reflect their differences. Staghorn Sumac's upper branches are covered with red-brown hairs, giving them a velvety appearance much like the velvet stage of a deer's antlers. The scientific name of this Sumac, *typhina,* refers to the genus *Typha,* or Cattails; with a little imagination, it is easy to see that the furry branches look like the matured brown seedheads on Cattails in winter. As you might expect, Smooth Sumac has no hairs on its upper branches. It is somehow comforting to have plants that are so reliably distinguishable from each other.

The inconspicuous flowers of this group of Sumacs usually go unnoticed by humans. Greenish white and borne in a large conical cluster, the blooms are unisexual and the sexes are generally borne on separate plants. If you get near the plants in bloom on a sunny day, you are bound to hear an undertone of buzzing. Honeybees are attracted in great numbers to the flowers, whose faint but pleasant odor reminds me a little of the smell of cake batter.

Almost all wild-food books describe the use of Sumac to make a refreshing drink. The outer coating of its fruit contains ascorbic acid, which can be leached out by soaking the fruits in water. What these books never mention is that the fruit clusters are also superb homes for insects. This past fall, while looking for some seedheads with which to make sumac-ade, I discovered that the fruits are favored by a particular small insect larva, probably that of a moth. If you break the seedheads open, you will often find five to ten of these larvae in a single cluster of the seeds. They are light purple, about a half inch long, and seem to feed on the fruits, leaving a trail

Staghorn Sumac fruits
in late summer

SUMAC

of droppings and silk behind. Since I do not want to add these ingredients to my sumac-ade, I have given up on the drink for this fall.

Even though this group of Sumacs produces its fruits in fall, I often find a high percentage of them still present on the plants through winter and into spring. I concluded that they were not eaten at all by birds, but was later proved wrong by a friend, who directed me to a shrub outside her window. There, on the tops of Staghorn Sumac, were Blue Jays and Chickadees, picking off the fruits. The Starlings and Robins that overwinter in northern areas are also reported to eat the fruits. It is interesting that the fruits of Poison Ivy and Poison Sumac disappear from their plants much faster than do those of other species. Their fruits are white and are eaten to a significant extent by many species of songbirds—among them, Catbirds, Flickers, Thrushes, and Chickadees.

On a late winter walk in Vermont, I once spotted some Smooth Sumac growing at the edge of an old field. The individual plants were large, with trunks as thick as three inches in diameter. On one of the plants, about four feet up its trunk, was a strange white patch. I waded through the waist-high

Flowers of Smooth Sumac

Staghorn Sumac in winter with birds

snow to get a closer look. The white area turned out to be a portion of gnawed-away bark, and from the size of the tooth marks, I was fairly sure it was the work of a Meadow Vole or Deer Mouse. I had often seen bark gnawed off a Multiflora Rose, but it had always been at the base of the plant. Clearly, the hungry animal had to climb up into the Sumac to get at this bark; perhaps the lower segment was too old and thick.

There are two signs of insect activity that can be detected on these sumacs in fall and winter. Especially on the branches of Smooth Sumac, you may see numerous pinhead-sized black dots arranged around the bark contours and often encircling lenticels or leaf scars. These are the waxy shells of Scale insects, or *Coccidae.* The shells are often secreted by the female and used as a protective cover as she moves about and feeds or when she hibernates through the winter. Also examine the tips of Sumac twigs; if any are broken off and have the pith hollowed, they may have been used by solitary wasps as brood chambers. See "Elderberry" for more details on the lives of the wasps.

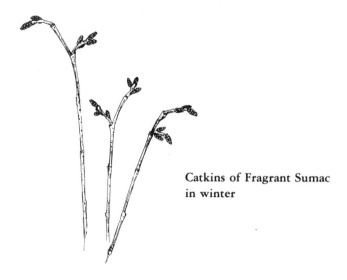

Catkins of Fragrant Sumac
in winter

The second group of Sumacs has only one member in eastern North America, Fragrant Sumac. What is striking about this species is how similar in appearance its leaves are to those of Poison Ivy. It is also unique among our native Sumacs in several respects. First, it is our only Sumac to have catkins. These are present all through winter in small clusters at the tips of the twigs. They bloom in early spring, and in summer ripen into small groups of fuzzy red fruits. The common and the scientific name *(aromatica)* of this plant reflect the fact that both the leaves and the catkins are scented. You can often fool friends by asking them to identify Fragrant Sumac. They almost always immediately say that it is Poison Ivy. At this point you bravely rub your hands across the leaves and then enjoy the smell they have left on your skin. Your friends will stare in amazement. Of course, *you* may end up staring in amazement if you find no fragrance on your hands and see that the plant actually is Poison Ivy.

The third group of Sumacs is comprised of the poisonous varieties; in eastern North America these include Poison Ivy, Poison Sumac, and Poison Oak. All members of this group differ from the other Sumacs in that they bear white to greenish fruits off the sides of their branches (unlike the red fruits produced at the tips of the branches of the other species). The

SUMAC

old adage regarding these shrubs is "Leaves three, then flee; berries white, take flight." Clearly, if you followed this to the letter, you would miss out on a lot of plants in the woods that are absolutely harmless—but you would also be certain not to get a case of the itchy blisters that are caused by contact with any part of these Sumacs in any season of the year. Someone occasionally makes the mistake of burning the wood of one of these species, with the result that its toxic resins become volatile and make broad contact with the person's skin.

Of the three poisonous species, Poison Ivy is the most ubiquitous and variable in form, growing as a sprawling vine, a thin upright shrub, or a thick tree-climbing vine secured to its support by a tangle of aerial roots. In all three guises, the plant is strangely alluring, its leaves tempting to touch in summer when they are shiny, or to collect in autumn, when they turn brilliant colors. Poison Ivy can be distinguished from the other Sumacs by its aerial roots and by fruits and flowers borne on lateral stems.

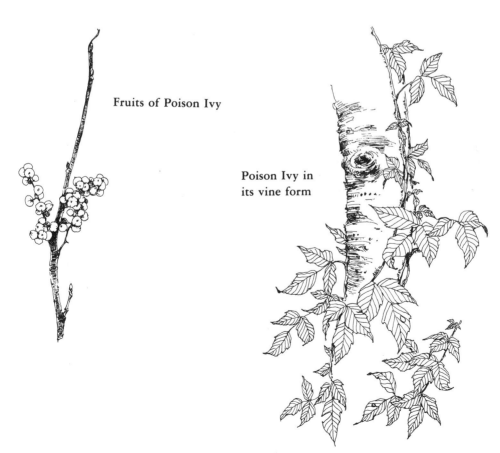

Fruits of Poison Ivy

Poison Ivy in
its vine form

SUMAC

Because it tends to grow in bogs or boglike habitats, Poison Sumac is far less common than Poison Ivy. It has very few branches on any given plant and often grows as high as fifteen feet or more. Its white fruits are carried on long racemes that grow off the sides of the branches a few inches behind the tip. I find that this species is the one most likely to give me a rash. I tend not to be on the lookout for it, and it is not conspicuous in summer, when at first glance you might mistake it for a sapling Ash tree. Poison Oak is similar to Poison Ivy, except that it is always an erect shrub and never a vine with aerial roots. It can grow to ten feet and is most often found in dry, sandy areas.

On the whole, the advantages of the Sumacs seem to outweigh their less agreeable aspects, especially if one heeds the slightly overcautious adage I cited earlier. Definitely on the positive side are the red-berried Sumacs, which produce greenery and wildlife food at the fringes of human spaces. In September, their large leaves soon turn to brilliant scarlet creating some of the earliest patches of color in the autumn landscape.

Fruits and leaves
of Poison Sumac

HOLLY

Ilex

ORDER: *Sapindales.*   FAMILY: *Aquifoliaceae.*   GENUS: *Ilex.*
SPECIES: *I. opaca,* American Holly; *I. vomitoria,* Cassina;
I. montana, Mountain Holly; *I. decidua,* Possum Haw;
I. verticillata, Winterberry; *I. glabra,* Inkberry;
I. coriacea, Large Gallberry, and others.

AN INVIGORATING FALL and winter sight in New England is the leafless branches of Winterberry Holly weighed down with their waxy red fruits. The plants are especially common along the coast, but can also be found inland at the edges of swamps and rivers and lakes. Winterberry is one of the most common Hollies in the East and yet I find that very few people know this plant or take time to enjoy it in winter. Northerners don't realize that they have native Hollies; when the genus is mentioned to Southerners, they think of American Holly, with its prickly evergreen leaves. But many species of Hollies grow the length of the eastern half of North America—some evergreen, some deciduous, some with red fruits, some with black fruits, some as shrubs, and others more commonly as trees.

In the northeastern United States, only three species of native Hollies are shrubs. One of these is Winterberry Holly, which is also known by the horribly confusing name of Black Alder. Although the plant is in no way related to the Alders (genus *Alnus*), it often grows in many of the same areas, such as near water. True Alders have neither petaled flowers nor fleshy fruits, but rather catkins and dry fruits produced in a small cone. Another deciduous Holly in the north, which also has red berries, is the Mountain Holly. It can always be easily distinguished from Winterberry Holly by the presence of short spur twigs on its branches. The spurs grow only a fraction of an inch each year; flowers and fruits are borne at their tips in tight clusters. Inkberry, the third northern species, is evergreen, but

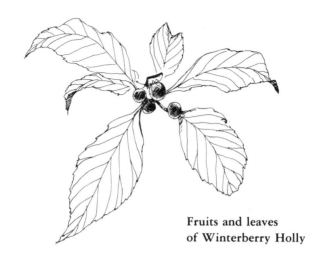

Fruits and leaves
of Winterberry Holly

looks less like our normal conception of Holly than even the genus's other deciduous species. Its leaves are small and lanceolate, dark green on top and lighter underneath. The plant tends to be only four or five feet high and very bushy. Its name may reflect the fact that its berries are not red like those of many other Hollies, but black. The male flowers of this species are borne in clusters; the female flowers grow singly, one in each leaf axil, so the black fruits also appear singly in the same position.

These three northern species also grow in the south, where they are joined by a host of other shrub species of Holly; in general, the Hollies seem to prefer the warmer climates. Large Gallberry is in most respects very similar to Inkberry, and the two are believed to be closely related. Large Gallberry differs in that its fruits are pulpy and borne in groups of one to five, instead of singly, like those of Inkberry. Its leaves also have short bristles near their tip, while those of Inkberry have only rounded indentations. Large Gallberry and Inkberry are our only two Holly species that are evergreen and have black berries.

A few common species of southern shrub Hollies are red-berried evergreens. Most of these live in southern coastal areas along the Atlantic Ocean and the Gulf of Mexico. The best known of these species is Cassina, or Yaupon. It is a large shrub, or sometimes a small tree, with small, shiny evergreen leaves that have rounded indentations all along their margins. Its bright-red fruits are borne in tight clusters immediately next to the

HOLLY

branches. Cassina is famous for the caffeine in its leaves and for the good-tasting tea that can be made from them. The leaves must be dried until they are black and crumbly; they can then be steeped in hot water just like Oriental tea. The leaves of both Large Gallberry and Inkberry can also be used to make tea in the same way. One species of Holly from South America is the source of the famous tea called Yerba Maté. The specific scientific name for Cassina is *vomitoria,* a reference to what happens if you attempt to eat the berries of this species, instead of making tea with its leaves.

Another widespread southern species is called Possum Haw, the same common name that is used for a species of Viburnum. Possum Haw is a deciduous plant with red fruits, and rather than staying near the coast like many southern species, it frequents the low moist land by rivers. Here you may find it joined by Winterberry Holly, which also grows well in these areas.

The flowers of all Hollies are unisexual. Both sexes may sometimes appear to be present in a particular bloom, but in these cases one is nonfunc-

Hollies: left, Inkberry; right, American Holly

tional. The flowers are small, greenish white, and either borne in the axils of the leaves or on short spurs. The fruits ripen by late summer and provide a significant source of food for wildlife. Thirty-five species of birds and mammals are known to feed on the fruits, and deer browse the foliage. In addition to their value as a food source, the evergreen Hollies provide valuable cover during the winter.

Holly is intimately linked in most of our minds with Christmas decorations. Only the evergreen species with red fruits (for the most part, American Holly and Cassina) are brought indoors at this time of year. This custom originated in pre-Christian ceremonies that celebrated the winter solstice. The bright fruits and shiny leaves were exchanged with friends and undoubtedly helped cheer up their houses at the time of year when daylight was at its shortest. When the later Christian festival of Christmas fell at almost the same time of year, the folk tradition was retained. So our enjoyment of Holly in midwinter actually has its roots in human awareness of the solar season and the rebirth of light, an awareness that is also carried over into the Christian story of the Nativity.

Flowers of Winterberry Holly

EUONYMUS

Euonymus

ORDER: *Sapindales.*   FAMILY: *Celastraceae.*   GENUS: *Euonymus.*
SPECIES: *E. atropurpureus,* Burning Bush;
E. fortunei, Wintercreeper; *E. europaeus,* European Spindle Tree;
E. alatus, Winged Euonymus; *E. americanus,* Strawberry Bush;
E. obovatus, Running Strawberry Bush.

SOME OF THE SPECIES of Euonymus that grow in eastern North America are so different from each other that you might at first think they were unrelated. Their fruits vary in color and shape; their flowers have different colors, arrangements, and numbers of petals and sepals; their leaves may be evergreen or deciduous; and the plants themselves may grow as vines, trailing shrubs, or small upright trees. The features common to the species —the characteristics that justify their being considered members of a single genus—are the general structure of their flowers and fruits, their four-sided twigs, and their paired leaves.

The flowers of all Euonymus species seem extremely simple in their construction. At their center is a small, slightly lobed, fleshy disk. Inserted around the edge of the disk are the stamens; in its center, either at the surface or on a very short style, is the stigma. This central disk secretes nectar and attracts mostly short-tongued bees and flies. After reading about the complex flowers of Dutchman's-Pipe and Sweetshrub, you might well wonder why insects go to so much trouble to obtain their food when a flower can be as easily accessible as that of Euonymus. There is no simple answer to this question, and in fact, Euonymus is not really as simple as it seems. It has its own pollination strategy, one that you can see in a slightly different form in the flowers of Pepperbush and Spirea. Although the flowers are bisexual, the male and female parts of the bloom mature at different times, so that at any given moment, the flower is functionally

EUONYMUS

unisexual. Because its male parts mature first, Euonymus is called *proterandrous.* Flowers like Spirea that mature female parts first are termed *proterogynous.*

Euonymus flowers develop into unusual fruits, one of the most beautiful aspects of these plants. The fruits are enclosed in a capsule that is called an aril. The aril varies in form among the different species: in some, it looks like a piece of popcorn; in others, more like the exterior of a Sycamore buttonball. As they grow, the fruits seem to burst from the top of the aril, but actually remain attached to it. This structure is characteristic for fruits

Euonymus twigs and fruits:
left, Winged Euonymus;
right, Burning Bush

of the entire *Celastraceae* family, of which Bittersweet is also a member.

There are about six species of Euonymus commonly found in eastern North America. The three native species—Burning Bush, Strawberry Bush, and Running Strawberry Bush—live primarily just inland from the coast, and range from Canada down to the Gulf states. But because both the native and the introduced species are widely used as ornamentals, they may be found growing in woods near any populated area.

One of the easiest Euonymus species to recognize is Winged Euonymus. All the plant's most recent twigs are lined with thin, bladelike, corky ridges on four sides. On the older branches, the corky material seems to break off, and the ridges are less prominent. No other common shrub in the East has this unusual characteristic, so Winged Euonymus can be quickly and surely identified in all seasons. I always wonder how and why these ridges evolved and whether there are other plants with similar features in eastern Asia, the region from which Winged Euonymus originally came. In fall, Winged Euonymus's leaves turn translucent pink and its fruits are red with purple arils. Framed in green twigs, the lovely hues make the plant particularly beautiful in this season.

Two native Euonymus species, Strawberry Bush and Running Strawberry Bush, are best recognized by their green, clearly four-sided twigs and unique fruits. Their common names probably refer to the appearance of the fruits, whose arils are about the size and shape of strawberries. Another common name for both species is Bursting Heart—the bright-orange fruits inside the arils do seem to have just burst out of their covering. These species are generally distinguished from each other by the shape of their leaves. Those of Running Strawberry Bush are widest near the tip, while those of Strawberry Bush are more evenly lanceolate. Running Strawberry Bush also tends to grow as a trailing shrub.

Two other like species are the native Burning Bush and the introduced Spindle Tree. The arils of both resemble pieces of popcorn attached to long, thin stalks. The arils of Burning Bush are scarlet and its fruits are purple; the arils of Spindle Tree are orange and its fruits pink. Both are upright shrubs and have an elegant symmetry to their branching that is particularly apparent in winter. The design is created by the paired branches growing off alternate sides of the square twigs. The older stems of Burning Bush have beautiful tan lines that trail off the leaf scars and continue longitudinally. Burning Bush is an extremely hardy plant and is often planted along roadsides or highways. Look for it in these areas in fall, when its leaves turn a bright red—a characteristic that explains the shrub's common name. Burning Bush is often in the company of Sumac and Bittersweet. Together, these three plants create a very colorful fall scene.

The last member of Euonymus is Wintercreeper, which has been introduced from Europe. It has several unique features. First, its thick, glossy leaves remain green through winter; second, it always grows as a vine; third, it climbs by aerial rootlets that grow directly from the sides of the new green stems. Its fruit is orange, covered by a smooth white aril. Because of its attractive fruits and evergreen leaves, it is often planted around buildings and in other landscaped areas. From these locations it is dispersed by birds that eat its fruits, so it may also be found growing wild nearby.

On the twigs of Euonymus, especially those of Wintercreeper, you are likely to find clusters of small Scale insects belonging to the order *Homoptera*. These insects secrete waxy coatings over their bodies for protection. The females look like minute mussel shells, while the males, which are smaller, appear to be just thin white marks on the vine. They live off juices that they suck from the stems of the plant. The most common species seen on Euonymus is *Chionaspis euonymi*.

The name Euonymus, which means "good plant," is a misnomer if applied to the genus's edibility. The seeds, leaves, and twigs of many species contain toxins which have caused the death of livestock that have fed upon them. But certainly its name is appropriate if used in reference to its ornamental qualities. Euonymus's beauty is apparent in fall, when the leaves of Winged Euonymus and Burning Bush turn translucent pink or deep scarlet, and when the fruits of all species show their orange-to-purple colors from within the varied shapes of their arils.

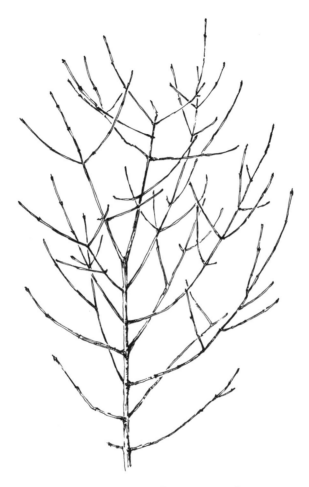

Winter twigs of Burning Bush

BITTERSWEET

Celastrus

ORDER: *Sapindales.* FAMILY: *Celastraceae.* GENUS: *Celastrus.*
SPECIES: *C. scandens,* American Bittersweet;
C. orbiculatus, Oriental Bittersweet.

A HOUSE THAT I moved into a few years ago had Bittersweet growing up a trellis on its front porch. Although the vine was then woody and leafless, I could easily imagine the colorful scene it would present the following fall when the berries had ripened to red and split their yellow casings. I watched the leaves expand, the flower buds grow, and the flowers open. Insects buzzed about the blooms, and I felt sure that lots of pollination was taking place and anticipated a good crop of berries. Then, in midsummer, all the flowers suddenly started to fall off. I was puzzled and could only guess that some disease had struck the plant. Later, when I took some time to learn the basic botany of Bittersweet, I was surprised to find that it is dioecious, that is, having unisexual flowers that are borne on separate plants. My vine was healthy; it just happened to be male.

Most people are familiar with Bittersweet in fall and winter, when it is a tough, woody vine with colorful fruits. But in spring and summer, the plant has an entirely different character and is easily overlooked. In spring, Bittersweet grows long green stems that twine around whatever their sensitive tips touch. Sometimes a number of new stems will twine about each other, forming a braided vine that supports itself as it reaches out into space. At other times, when the growing tip touches the branch of a shrub or tree, its new growth spirals up around the shrub's or tree's branches and trunk. In this way it climbs toward the sun without the aid of tendrils or aerial roots. Other vines that climb in this manner include: Wisteria, Honeysuckle, Dutchman's-Pipe, and Moonseed. Bittersweet's method of climbing presents one interesting problem in that once the vine has wrapped itself snugly around a branch, there is no room for either to expand in circumference as it grows. The usual result is that the vine presses into the branch and the wood of the branch begins to grow around the vine, eventually embedding it. When the vine dies and falls away, the spiraling scar remains as a clue to its former presence.

While looking for Bittersweet in midsummer, you may find a plant that is very similar to it except that it has the added characteristic of black thorns. If you touch one of these thorns, it will do one of two things: it will either disappear before your eyes, or move around to the other side of the vine. The plant is indeed Bittersweet, but what appear to be thorns are actually insects called Two-marked Treehoppers, *Enchenopa binotata.* In late summer and fall, the adult females make a small slit on the bark of the vine, in which they lay their eggs. They then cover over the area with a sticky white substance that looks and feels like the center of marshmallows. The substance is placed over the eggs in layers, much like the casing over Praying Mantis eggs. The eggs remain this way through winter. The young, which hatch the following summer, feed on the juices of the new twigs. Some observers have said that the insects always line up in the same direction along the vine, a trait that may have evolved to make them look more like real thorns. This is a nice idea, but from my own observations, I find the bugs far more individualistic in their behavior.

Bittersweet branches
twining about each other

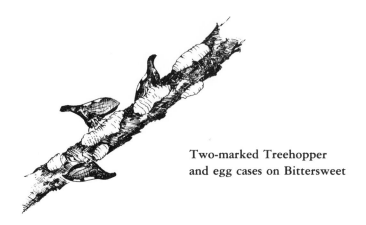

Two-marked Treehopper
and egg cases on Bittersweet

There are two common species of Bittersweet—the native American Bittersweet and the imported Oriental Bittersweet. Except for the placement of the fruits, the two are quite similar. In the American Bittersweet, the fruits are borne only at the tips of the twigs, while in the Oriental plant,

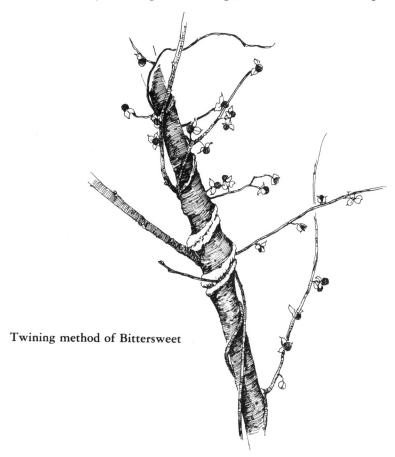

Twining method of Bittersweet

BITTERSWEET

they grow along the sides of the twigs in small clusters. The two species also differ in the color of their arils, the coating around the red fruit. In our native species it is orange; in the introduced variety it is tan or light yellow.

It is certainly tempting to gather the fruiting branches of Bittersweet in fall and bring them indoors to brighten up a mantelpiece or holiday table, but I am afraid that because we now live in a different age, we can no longer do so without some thought. I know that in my own area, none of the few large stands of Bittersweet are the native species. I have looked hard for American Bittersweet and found only one small scraggly vine far back in the woods. It is thought that this scarcity of American Bittersweet is the result of extensive picking of the fruits for private and commercial purposes. Clearly we have the ability to wipe out a species of plant within a period of a few years, not only because the human population is larger, but also because there are fewer places where the plants can grow. Since Audubon's time, when birds were routinely killed for study, we have changed our ethics, and birds are now protected. We must similarly become more aware of plants and no longer automatically pick them for our brief use. We must be more thoughtful and aware of our plant environment. Learn the difference between American Bittersweet and Oriental Bittersweet, and never pick from the one that is less common in your area. When gathering, take just enough fruits or flowers to enjoy, so that the plant can continue its normal life patterns and remain a beautiful sight for all those who pass by on their winter walks.

Winter fruits of
Oriental Bittersweet

BUCKTHORN

Rhamnus

ORDER: *Rhamnales.*   FAMILY: *Rhamnaceae.*   GENUS: *Rhamnus.*
SPECIES: *R. alnifolia,* Alder-leaved Buckthorn;
R. cathartica, Common Buckthorn;
R. lanceolata, Lance-leaved Buckthorn;
R. caroliniana, Carolina Buckthorn;
R. Frangula, European Buckthorn.

GROWING AS HIGH as fifteen feet and with just a single main trunk, buckthorns generally look more like small trees than shrubs. They can be found flourishing in both the understory of open woods and along the sunny edges of roads, fields, and forests. Although three native species of Buckthorn grow in eastern North America, two other species, introduced from Europe, are rapidly becoming the most common. Of the native species, Carolina Buckthorn and Lance-leaved Buckthorn grow mostly in the south, while Alder-leaved Buckthorn grows primarily in the north. The introduced species, European Buckthorn and Common Buckthorn, overlap the ranges of the natives, and while especially common in the north, they are steadily extending their range south as well. Why these introduced plants, which in most ways are similar to our native varieties, can do so well that they outpace the indigenous species is an intriguing question that has yet to be studied carefully in this genus.

The different Buckthorns vary considerably in the structure of their flowers. The Carolina and European Buckthorns have bisexual flowers with five petals and five stamens. Lance-leaved Buckthorn's flowers are also bisexual but have only four petals and four stamens; furthermore, its flowers appear in two distinct forms: in one, the pistil protrudes from the flower, while in the other, it remains retracted. Individual plants of this

§ 144

species will have either one or the other of these flower forms, but never both. Bisexual and unisexual flowers are found on the Common and Alder-leaved Buckthorns; while Common Buckthorn's flowers have four petals and four stamens, those of Alder-leaved Buckthorn have no petals at all.

All species of Buckthorn start to blossom in May and are visited frequently by bees and flies that come to feed on the nectar. While most species end their blooming in June, the Alder-leaved and European Buckthorns keep producing flowers through most of the summer. This habit makes them especially colorful in the warmer months, when their branches hold a mixture of green flower buds, white opened flowers, red immature fruits, and black ripe fruits.

Because none of their features are particularly outstanding, Buckthorns can be fairly anonymous plants in summer. But in fall and winter, the form and abundance of their fruits distinguishes them from most other trees and shrubs. All Buckthorn fruits are fleshy drupes that turn black when ripe and contain two to four hardened nutlets. In some species, the fruits are borne on short stalks that grow directly out of the twigs, often looking as if they were just glued to the branch. The fruits of other species seem more naturally placed, growing from the leaf axils or from the tips of short spurs.

The fruits of Carolina Buckthorn are reportedly sweet and edible, ac-

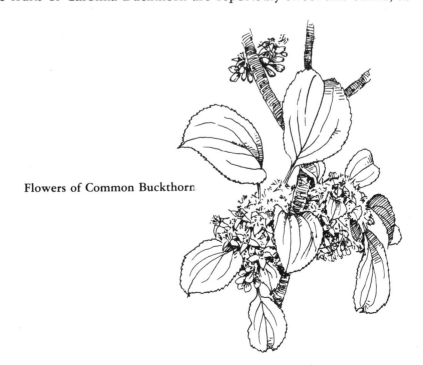

Flowers of Common Buckthorn

counting for the plant's other common name, Indian Cherry. But before you try to eat them, be sure that you can distinguish this species from the similar European and Alder-leaved Buckthorns, both of which have bad-tasting fruits. Common Buckthorn's fruits are known to be a strong laxative, as its Latin species name, *cathartica,* suggests. Although not used as food, they are the source of a green dye called Chinese Green.

In fall, I am often asked the name of a shrub that has thorns at the tips of its branches. This plant is Common Buckthorn, the only member of the genus with this characteristic. The species is particularly interesting to visit in winter, when its branching pattern and the placement of its buds can be easily observed. Look at the shrub and you will see basically two angles of branching. Twigs that grow off the sides of main branches form almost 90-degree angles with them, making the plant very geometric. A different angle of branching occurs at the tips of twigs that end in thorns. Here, the two buds just below the thorn take over, branching off at about 30 degrees and forming a Y with the thorn of the original twig at its center. These branching patterns give the shrub a sharp, angular appearance, making it seem as if you could easily draw the plant with just a protractor and ruler. The arrangement of Common Buckthorn's buds is also unusual. If you look at the tips of the twigs, you will see the leaf buds in pairs, one on either

Fruits and leaves of Common Buckthorn

Buckthorn twigs:
left, European Buckthorn;
right, Common Buckthorn

Twigs and spines
of Common Buckthorn

side of the twig. This may lead you to believe that Common Buckthorn always has opposite buds. But farther back on the twigs, you will find that the buds gradually become out of phase and finally alternate. Common Buckthorn is the only shrub or vine in eastern North America that frequently has this characteristic.

In winter, the Carolina and European Buckthorns are easily differentiated from the other species by their naked buds; in other words, their preformed leaves for the coming year are not enclosed in protective scales. The buds are about a quarter of an inch long and resemble a cluster of minute withered leaves. This peculiarity is shared by only a few other common shrubs or vines, including Hobblebush, Poison Ivy, and Witch Hazel.

§ 147 §

NEW JERSEY TEA

Ceanothus

ORDER: *Rhamnales.*   FAMILY: *Rhamnaceae.*   GENUS: *Ceanothus.*
SPECIES: *C. americanus,* New Jersey Tea; *C. ovatus,* Redroot.

NEW JERSEY TEA is one of the least known of our native eastern shrubs, possibly because its fine, open-branched stems are rarely more than three feet tall. The plants also live in sunny "edge" habitats, where their clusters of minute white blossoms are easily outclassed by more showy roadside flowers. I first collected a sample of New Jersey Tea one winter when I was out looking for the dried seed stalks of summer flowers—what I call "winter weeds." At first I thought it was the dried remains of a wildflower, since the entire plant was only two feet tall and had delicate branching. I brought it home to identify, and not finding it in any of my wildflower books, I checked a guide to shrubs and soon learned by the distinctive appearance of its dried seeds that it was New Jersey Tea.

The seeds develop at the ends of a few thin branches that are connected to the main stem by a long, straight stalk. At the tip of each separate branch are three black-coated seeds arranged in thirds, like the shape of a home-made roll. After the black coating is shed (apparently during fall or into winter), the seeds or nutlets appear white; as they dry, they are forcibly expelled off the seedhead, so that what remains on the top of each small branch are beautiful silver-white disks. As you lean close to see them, you will discover what an exquisite pattern the disks make. New Jersey Tea is well worth a visit, and in winter I always stop at a spot near me where I know they grow. Although I occasionally collect a stem to put in a vase on my desk and enjoy while I work, I often hesitate to do so, since unlike the stems of winter weeds, which are dead in winter, those of New Jersey Tea are still green under their bark and will continue to live for several years.

One of the most puzzling aspects of New Jersey Tea is the shape of its flowers. Each of the five little petals that project out of the center of a blossom looks like a miniature ladle, with a narrow base that broadens rapidly at its tip, forming a small cup. The many bees I have watched come to the flowers seemed to have no unusual interaction with these petals, so whether their odd shape has a function remains a mystery to me.

Once, while examining a showy cluster of New Jersey Tea flowers, I spotted a Crab Spider, a common spider whose two front pairs of legs are particularly long and are held in a position similar to the way a crab holds its pincers. Except for the red marking on its back, the spider was just the color of the white New Jersey Tea blossoms. This coloring is essential to it, because instead of making a web like some spiders to catch prey, or running after victims like Wolf Spiders, the Crab Spider rests motionless, camouflaged in a spot where insects will come to it. The flowers of New Jersey Tea were obviously serving their purpose, for as I looked closer I discovered that the spider had already caught a small Honeybee.

The name New Jersey Tea refers to the use of the leaves during colonial times as a substitute for the teas that were then being imported from England. This practice was especially common during the time of the tea embargo, when it was considered unpatriotic to drink English tea. In the north was another shrub whose leaves could be used, Labrador Tea, but

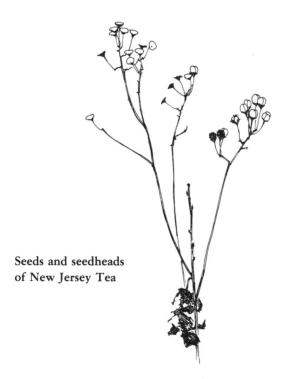

Seeds and seedheads
of New Jersey Tea

Flowers and leaves
of New Jersey Tea

in the south, New Jersey Tea was more common. A few years ago, when I first learned about the plant, I wanted to try making the tea for myself, to see what it really tasted like. I gathered a bunch of leaves and let them dry on one corner of my desk for about a month, until they became extremely brittle. I put them into a teapot with about a cup and a half of boiling water. As I waited for the tea to steep, I started reviewing the uses of the plant in wild-food books. Gradually I became aware of a pleasant new odor in the kitchen, coming from the teapot. I poured some tea out into a white cup; it was a light greenish brown, like an Oriental tea. All the natural-foods books had advised that it would taste better with cream and sugar (what doesn't?), so I prepared myself as I took a sip of the tea without additives. It was good—mild but with body, very much like some of the teas served at Chinese restaurants. I took the pot and cup up to my study and found the second cup especially good, though the third was quite strong, and had a bit of a bite.

If you dig down at the base of any group or cluster of New Jersey Tea stems, you are likely to find a thick gnarl of roots. These are larger and heavier than the aerial stems, because each of the stems lives for only a few years, while the roots remain living much longer and continue to send up new shoots. The roots of New Jersey Tea are a deep red and can be used to make a good dye. This trait accounts for another common name of the species—Redroot.

NEW JERSEY TEA

The roots of *Ceanothus* are known to associate with certain bacteria and form nitrogen-fixing nodules, and so the plants can be considered to perform some service in enriching the soil in which they grow. While many legumes are known to have this ability, relatively few other non-legumes possess it. Among those that do are several other shrub species: Sweet Gale, Sweet Fern, and Alder.

Growing best in dry, rich soil, New Jersey Tea has a very wide range. While our two species in the East are never very common, the western species are often the dominant shrubs in certain areas. The western shrub *C. velutinus,* generally known as Snowbush, is especially widespread and valuable as browse for grazing animals. Some other western species, such as Spiny Ceanothus and Blue Blossom, even grow to tree size. Although these species differ from our smaller eastern shrubs in having evergreen leaves and blue flowers, they do share with eastern plants a common structure and arrangement of flowers and fruits.

One fall while I was heading out to draw plants, I noticed some bird droppings on the top of the posts of a bridge. They were dry and obviously full of seeds. I looked closely at the seeds and drew a small sketch of a few of them. Later on my walk, I happened to pick some seeds off the stalks of New Jersey Tea, and was surprised and pleased to discover that they were the same shape as those in the bird droppings. Some species of bird obviously eats the seeds of New Jersey Tea, and is helping to disperse this lovely plant across the countryside.

Branching of New Jersey Tea

VIRGINIA CREEPER

Parthenocissus

ORDER: *Rhamnales.* FAMILY: *Vitaceae.* GENUS: *Parthenocissus.*
SPECIES: *P. quinquefolia,* Virginia Creeper;
P. inserta, Thicket Creeper; *P. tricuspidata,* Boston Ivy.

VIRGINIA CREEPER has a method of climbing that is unique among eastern vines. Instead of using tendrils as Grape and Greenbrier do, or twining as Honeysuckle and Bittersweet do, the plant has small branching tendrils that form adhesive disks at their tips when they come into contact with something to which they can attach. Because the disks are formed only after the tendrils touch a support, tendrils that never establish such a contact do not develop adhesive disks, but instead curl about themselves. The disks are very small—only about an eighth of an inch in diameter—but have an amazing ability to hold fast at their point of attachment. It has been estimated that a single tendril with just five disk-bearing branches could support up to ten pounds.

Discovering adhesive disks on a vine in the wild will assure you that you have discovered either Virginia Creeper or its close introduced relative, Boston Ivy. But one other species in this genus, Thicket Creeper, has no disks on its tendrils. In eastern North America, Thicket Creeper is found mostly in Canada, but farther west, its range extends southward, so that at the West Coast it grows in Arizona and up through California. Both Virginia Creeper and Thicket Creeper have compound leaves, usually composed of five leaflets (the scientific name of Virginia Creeper, *quinquefolia,* means "five-leaved") joined to the petiole at a single point, forming the shape of a fan. This shape is often called palmately compound, since it resembles the fingers radiating from the palm of your hand. The long petiole is in turn attached to the woody stem.

If you come upon Virginia Creeper in midsummer, take some time to

VIRGINIA CREEPER

look over its leaflets and petioles, for this species is the main food plant of three of our most common Sphinx moths. Other discussions of Sphinx moths in this book (in the Honeysuckle and Rhododendron sections) have focused on the feeding habits of the nocturnal adults, which have long mouthparts with which they extract the nectar from long-tubed flowers. But the common name of the Sphinx moth derives from the larval habits of this insect: when the caterpillars are disturbed, they pull the front of their bodies up and back and look much like an Egyptian Sphinx in its sitting posture. Besides this characteristic pose, all Sphinx caterpillars have a thin pointed projection, sometimes called a "horn," on the top of their last body segment. In the later stages of their larval life, this horn shrinks and finally becomes a dot.

The larva of two species of Sphinx—the Myron Sphinx, *Ampeloeca myron,* and the Pandorus Sphinx, *Pholus pandorus*—are called Hog Caterpillars,

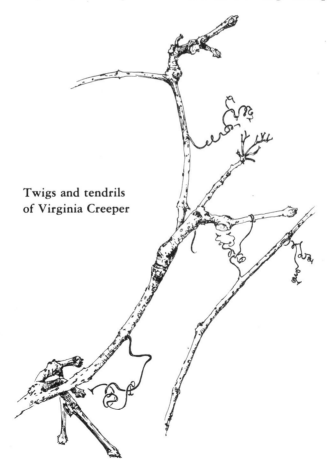

Twigs and tendrils
of Virginia Creeper

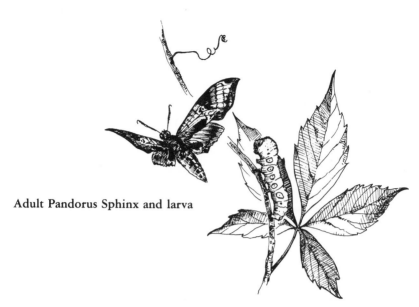

Adult Pandorus Sphinx and larva

due to their ability to retract the first two segments of their bodies back into the third segment, which gives them a hog-nosed appearance. The third species of this genus is the White-lined Sphinx, *Celerio lineata.* When searching for Sphinx larvae on Virginia Creeper, look for evidence of their feeding, such as chewed leaves or bits of excrement on leaf surfaces or on the ground beneath the plant.

In all three species of Sphinx, the adults emerge from their pupa in early summer and lay their eggs on Virginia Creeper, where the caterpillars will feed and grow. The caterpillars leave their food plant in late summer or early fall and work their way into the ground, where they transform into pupae and remain in that state through the winter. In early summer, the pupae work their way to the soil surface, where the adults emerge. The Myron Sphinx differs slightly from this pattern in that its larva does not burrow into the ground but forms a pupa among fallen leaves on the surface.

The small, inconspicuous flowers of Virginia Creeper are either bisexual or, occasionally, unisexual. In either case, both sexes of flowers exist on the same plant. Bees seem to be the most common insect visitors, and I have noticed that they continue to come to the flowers long after the petals have been shed. The flowers bloom from late June into August, and by fall the flower stalks have turned bright red; at their tips are dark-blue berries covered with a white powdery substance. The fruits provide valuable fall

VIRGINIA CREEPER

and winter food for many songbirds, including the Mockingbird, Robin, Brown Thrasher, Wood Thrush, and Pileated Woodpecker.

Along with the Sumacs, Virginia Creeper is one of our first plants whose leaves change color in the fall. The foliage turns to a marvelous shade of deep red that fades to a translucent light pink, so that when struck by the sun, the leaves light up and give off a rosy glow to the surrounding plants. The brilliant red of the vine is so distinctive and appears so much earlier than in most other plants that in early fall it is extremely easy to spot patches of the plant at great distances, or even as you drive along the road. Once, I found an area by the seacoast where every tree and shrub for acres was covered by Virginia Creeper. Obviously the plant was killing off most of the other vegetation by robbing it of sunlight, but it certainly was a beautiful sight, like a scarlet blanket of leaves laid across the landscape.

In winter, it is good to think twice before you touch vines of what you believe to be Virginia Creeper, for sometimes they can look very much like those of Poison Ivy. Certainly, if there are fruits, then you can easily distinguish the two, Poison Ivy's being white and Virginia Creeper's being blue. But if only the stems are visible and you cannot clearly see disks on the tendrils, then the plants can be easily confused. Although Poison Ivy has only aerial roots and no tendrils, it has such varied forms that its aerial roots may in fact be mistaken for tendrils. In any case, there is really not much reason to handle either plant in winter, and so I recommend that you wait until spring, when the graceful five-part leaves of Virginia Creeper will invite you to make further investigations without fear of getting a rash on your skin.

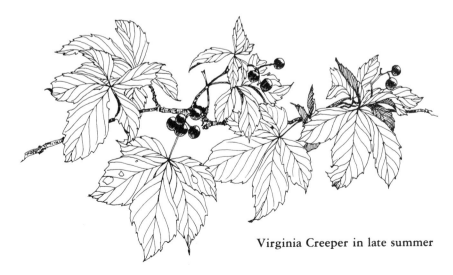

Virginia Creeper in late summer

GRAPE

Vitis

ORDER: *Rhamnales.*   FAMILY: *Vitaceae.*   GENUS: *Vitis.*
SPECIES: *V. Labrusca,* Fox Grape; *V. Aestivalis,* Summer Grape,
and many others.

WHEN I GO canoeing in fall on the slow, peaceful rivers near where I live,
I am always on the lookout for Grapes. The big trees—the Oaks, Silver
Maples, and Sycamores—that hang out over the river are often covered
with the long drooping vines. Somehow, these scenes always make me
imagine what the land must have been like early in North America's
history, when explorers traveled up the slow rivers, seeing many of the
same scenes, which then were probably only more tangled and lush. Even
with your eyes closed, you could find Grapes at this time of year, when the
scent of the fruit is strong. I usually approach the vines in my canoe and
then lift up the big leaves in search of the familiar blue clusters. They are
often so ripe that as soon as I even touch the vine a shower of Grapes plops
into the water. They get tossed into the center of the canoe, to be eaten
on the way back as I drift downstream.

The many species of Grapes are hard to distinguish, for their differences
are slight. In addition, the plants frequently hybridize, creating many inter-
mediate forms which blur the distinctions between species. The taste of the
fruits produced by wild Grape vines varies as much within species as
between species, so that there is really no way to predict whether the fruit
from a particular vine will be sweet or sour. In any case, most wild grapes
can be transformed into marvelous condiments with cooking and the addition of sugar. Jelly made from wild grapes is hard to beat and wild Grape
juice is also a winner. Even the tender, fully expanded leaves of our wild
species can be used to wrap rice and meat mixtures, just like the expensive
varieties you buy canned in stores.

GRAPE

One of the parts of Grape vines most frequently used by animals is the bark. On most species, it is finely lined longitudinally and peels off freely in lengthy strips. Many birds, especially Catbirds, Mockingbirds, Brown Thrashers, and Cardinals, use liberal amounts of Grape bark in the middle layer of their nests. The Cardinal uses the bark even more extensively. They gather long strips of about one-quarter inch in width that are already peeling off the vine naturally. Smaller birds gather the bark differently. The Purple Finch, for example, pulls off many thin strips with several quick motions, so that the accumulated bark has the quality of fine blades of grass. I have found strips of this size woven into the structure of Goldfinch nests as well.

I find Grape to be at its loveliest in spring, when its large leaf buds are just beginning to open. Colored with a shade of rose, the downy buds look like opening flowers. They are easily visible in the spring woods, since they open quite early in the season, before many leaves on other species of shrubs have emerged. Soon afterward, new shoots grow, along with beautiful split tendrils which support the vine by holding on to the parts of other plants. The tendrils have fascinating ways of twining around their supports, and are worth close observation. Their various methods of twisting are described in detail in the section on Greenbrier.

Riverbank Grape with fruits

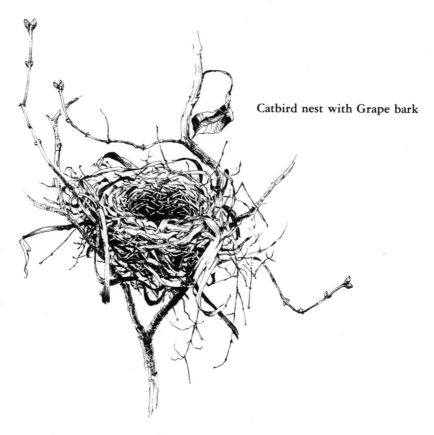

Catbird nest with Grape bark

Grape flowers are very fragrant but quite inconspicuous visually. Although both male and female parts are usually present in each flower, any given cluster may be functionally unisexual, with only one sex actually fertile. Generally, however, a single plant has both bisexual and unisexual flowers. One of the oddities of Grape flowers is the form of their petals. Each blossom ordinarily has five petals which are joined at their tips to form a little five-part cone over the sexual parts of the flower. While the petals of most flowers stay on the blossom as advertisement to pollinators, those of Grape must be shed before pollinators can even reach the sexual parts. It remains a curiosity how this structure came about in evolution and what purpose the petals now serve.

Grapes seem to be particularly attractive to insects, and by midsummer many galls can be discovered on the vines. The Grape Tomato Gall, made by the gall gnat *Lasioptera vitis,* is a swelling about the size of a pea, which can be found either on the tendril or on a vein of a leaf. On the base of the tendril may be an elongated swelling: this is also a gall, formed by the gall gnat *Asteromyia petiolicola.* A third common gall is the Grape Tube Gall. It is formed in the leaves, most often in clusters that look like little pointed caps on the leaf's upper surface. These are made by the gall gnat *Cecidomyia viticola,* and in midsummer you can often find the tiny larvae of these insects by carefully prying apart the galls. All gall gnats belong to the family of flies called *Cecidomyiidae.*

If you ever have occasion to enjoy a bottle of good California or French wine, take a moment to give thanks for our native American Grapes. There is a small plant louse called *Phylloxera vastratrix,* which lives in eastern North America. Although it is a simple, peaceful insect, at one point it was responsible for destroying over two million acres of French vineyards and for devastating the California wine industry as well. This tiny bug has a complicated two-year life cycle that alternates between the leaves and the roots of Grape vines. While it does not totally damage the leaves, it does

Grape flowers and tendrils

Ripened grapes

feed on and cause deformations in the roots, eventually killing them. Many of our wild vines were immune to this root damage, but as soon as the bug was accidentally carried to Europe, it wiped out the French plants, and since the domesticated vines in California were also of French origin, they too were hurt. The only solution was to graft the French vines that produced the best Grapes onto the roots of those American species that were resistant to plant lice. Evidence of the presence of *Phylloxera vastratrix* on the leaves is many small bumps (which contain wingless lice) on the leaf surface. On the roots, their work takes the form of elongated swellings.

I love the rich, almost musty smell of the well-ripened Grapes in late fall. The aroma especially advertises the presence of the fruit to mammals, who often depend on their sense of smell to locate food. Because of their large size and strong fermenting odor, Grapes are basically a mammal-dispersed fruit. One fall, near a large patch of Grape, I found fox scats composed entirely of hardly digested Grapes, with just the skins separated from the pulp. What a marvelous way to disperse seeds in new places, and what a trick on the fox, who is obviously strongly attracted by the smell, eats the Grapes off the vines, disperses the seeds, and yet receives hardly any nutrition in return for its effort. In this case, the animal is outfoxed by the Grape.

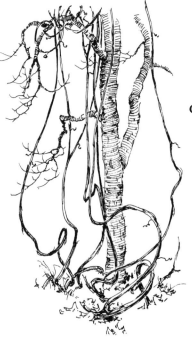

Grape vines in winter

HERCULES'-CLUB

Aralia

ORDER: *Umbelliflorae.*   FAMILY: *Araliaceae.*   GENUS: *Aralia.*
SPECIES: *A. spinosa,* Hercules'-Club.

IF YOU HAD to design a structure that could absorb sunlight, extract water and minerals from the earth, and protect itself from possible harm by animals, you probably could not come up with a simpler solution than Hercules'-Club. Although this plant can grow as high as thirty feet and have several branches, it is usually less than half that height, with just a single straight stem. Its leaves and flowers grow from the top end bud and radiate in all directions, making the plant look a little like a palm tree, and its stem is menacingly armed with sharp, strong thorns. The unbranched stem and thorns have obviously been the source of many of the shrub's common names, which include Devil's-Walking-Stick, Spikenard, Tearblanket, and the most often used, Hercules'-Club.

One advantage to vertical growth with no branching is that all new wood is added to height, thus overcoming the need to compete with other vegetation for sunlight. While its height is helpful to Hercules'-Club, which does particularly well in full sun, it is not essential, for the plant also thrives under partial shade and can be found even in the understory of older forests. Hercules'-Club spreads vigorously by rootstocks that send up numerous new shoots. If any damage occurs to the roots, the number of shoots the plant produces tends to increase.

A striking feature of Hercules'-Club in winter is its huge end bud. Inside this single bud are all the plant's leaves for the coming year. In spring, the bud is an exciting sight, its large scales pushed back by the emerging leaves, which seem to burst out like water starting from a fountain.

All plants must find a way to distribute their leaves efficiently in light. There are a number of methods to solve this problem. One is to have a

Emerging spring leaves
of Hercules'-Club

network of very fine branching that holds many small, simple leaves. Another is to have less elaborate branching, but compensate for it with large
compound leaves. The third solution is to have practically no branching,
but huge, twice-compound leaves. This last is the structure of Hercules'-
Club. Its twice-compound leaves, which all project from the tips of the
stem, are larger than those of any of our other shrubs or vines, and sometimes reach up to three feet in length.

Not only are the leaves of Hercules'-Club the largest among our common shrubs and vines; its clusters of flowers are too. The individual flowers
are tiny and grouped into small perfect umbels, which are in turn arranged
along a large compound panicle that may be as much as two feet long. The
flowers are greenish white, and though under different circumstances they
might be inconspicuous, as part of such large panicles they are quite showy.
The flowers are bisexual and develop into fleshy drupes that each contain
five hardened seeds. The fruits are eaten by only a few birds and mammals,
and no one animal eats them to any great extent. Another common name
for Hercules'-Club is Pigeonberry, or Pigeon Tree; whatever the reason
for this designation, you can be assured that it is not because Pigeons feed
extensively on the fruits.

HERCULES'-CLUB

It is easy to collect some of Hercules'-Club's panicles of fruits in fall and early winter, when the entire long cluster is shed from the shrub. It is a striking, colorful form; late in the year, the small fruits become black and the intricate stalk turns first purple and later a dusty brown. You will notice that the stalks of the individual fruits are radially arranged, like the spokes of a wheel. If their black coverings have fallen off, look closely at the fruits and you will see the five seeds matured from a single flower arranged like a miniature paddlewheel.

On the stems of Hercules'-Club are three types of plant scar, which, along with the thorns and some vertical fissures, make intricate patterns on the bark. One type of scar appears as an encircling ring of fine lines covering about an inch of trunk length. This same form of scar repeats at irregular intervals up and down the stem. These markings trace where the winter bud scales, sloughed off in spring, were attached to the plant. Each

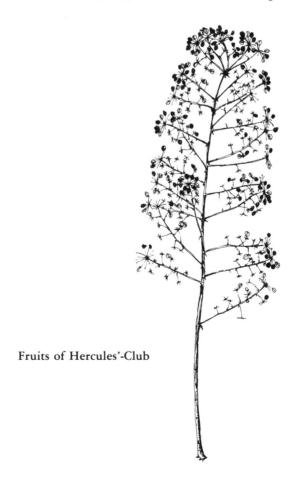

Fruits of Hercules'-Club

set of rings indicates a year of growth, thus enabling you to determine the age of the plant. Also on the stem are the large V-shaped leaf scars, marking where the leaves were attached. The many small dots within these scars are called bundle scars and are evidence of the main tubes that carried nutrients to the leaf. All woody plants have such markings on their branches and stems, but nowhere are they more easily seen than on Hercules'-Club.

The genus of Hercules'-Club, *Aralia,* has only a few other species in eastern North America. One of them is the common herbaceous plant Wild Sarsaparilla, *A. nudicaulis.* This plant has lovely compound leaves and small white flowers arranged in a spherical umbel when in bloom. The ranges of Wild Sarsaparilla and Hercules'-Club seem to complement each other. Wild Sarsaparilla grows mostly in the north, but extends farther south in the Appalachian Mountains; Hercules'-Club grows primarily in the south, but extends north in the lowlands along riverbanks. *Aralia* belongs to the family *Araliaceae,* which is often called the Ginseng family, since it includes the genus *Panax,* and its species *P. quinquefolium,* the native plant Ginseng. This plant has some notoriety, and because it grows a split root which makes the uprooted plant resemble a human form, it is believed to possess various powers and possible magic.

Scars and spines
of Hercules'-Club along
with Daddy Long-legs

DOGWOOD

Cornus

ORDER: *Umbelliflorae.*   FAMILY: *Cornaceae.*   GENUS: *Cornus.*
SPECIES: *C. stolonifera,* Red Osier Dogwood;
C. rugosa, Round-leaved Dogwood; *C. Amomum,* Swamp Dogwood;
C. racemosa, Gray-stemmed Dogwood, and others.

FOR MANY YEARS I thought the name Dogwood referred only to a flowering tree, and not until recently did I discover the many woody shrubs of the same family. These shrubs are surprisingly common, often dominating roadsides, meadows, and riverbanks. While attractive throughout the year, they are most striking in winter, when the colors and patterns of their leafless branches stand out, each species so distinct as to reveal its identity even from a distance. I enjoy these bare shrubs in winter as much as I do the flowering plants in spring, and rarely pass them without pausing to appreciate their colors, habits, and forms.

If you have never seen a Dogwood—tree or shrub—take heart, for the genus is easy to recognize, especially in winter. There are three common species of shrub, the most conspicuous being Red Osier Dogwood, which has bright fire-engine-red bark on its twigs and its upper branches. Swamp Dogwood always grows near water and has maroon twigs with fine silky hairs along their outermost portions. Both these species grow as clusters of stems that all sprout from the same spot. In contrast, Gray-stemmed Dogwood grows in close groves of individual plants. This species has smooth gray stems, at the tips of which are red panicles, where berries were attached in fall. All three shrubs tend to grow in open areas, their colors and growth patterns so obvious that they can be identified even from a passing car.

Gray-stemmed Dogwood always makes me think of birds' nests, since I

DOGWOOD

find more nests among its winter branches than those of any other shrub. This abundance is not just chance, but is a function of the distinctive characteristics of this species. Gray-stemmed Dogwood grows at the edges of meadows or in old fields, habitats where a great deal of insect and seed food attracts many common songbirds. Additionally, unlike the sprawling branches of other Dogwood shrubs, the fine upper twigs of Gray-stemmed Dogwood form a superb support for both the woven grass nests of Sparrows and the bulky nests of Catbirds and Mockingbirds. This Dogwood's usefulness as a nesting site is also due to its habit of growth. Starting as a single plant, it spreads by rootstocks which continually sprout new suckers toward areas with the most light. The groves that eventually form take on a characteristic shape—a gentle curve, rising from the younger plants at the edge to the taller, older plants at the center. The shrubs create islands of vegetation in meadows, and nests at their centers are virtually invisible,

Gray-stemmed Dogwood growing in an old field

Berries of Gray-stemmed Dogwood

their natural materials blending with the masses of silvery twigs. One winter, in a nearby field of only a few acres, I found nests of Goldfinch, Catbird, Mockingbird, Red-Wing Blackbird, Song Sparrow, and Chipping Sparrow—all constructed in Gray-stemmed Dogwood. I have yet to find a nest in any other native Dogwood shrub.

At the tips of Gray-stemmed Dogwood's upper branches you may find an enlarged portion the size of a marble. This is the Dogwood Bud Gall, caused by a gall gnat in the genus *Cecidomyia,* and it occurs only on this species. In winter, I have also had good luck locating cocoons on Gray-stemmed Dogwood. One I have found, a large, messy cocoon broadly attached to the larger branches, is the winter home of the Cecropia moth. Although the larva of this species does not have specific food plants, I have

From left to right:
Cecropia Moth cocoon,
Tussock Moth cocoon,
Dogwood Bud Gall

come across more of its cocoons on Gray-stemmed Dogwood than on any other shrub. A much more common cocoon is that of the White-marked Tussock moth, *Hermocampa leucostigma.* It can best be located by examining small leaves still attached to the winter twigs; some will undoubtedly have small cocoons within them. Sometimes a cocoon will have a hardened, frothy substance on it, indicating that it was inhabited by a female moth. She is wingless when she emerges from the cocoon and attracts a mate by releasing a scent. Once mated, she lays her eggs in a bubbly mass on her cocoon.

In winter, when the leaves have fallen from Gray-stemmed Dogwood and most of its berries have been eaten, only the panicles at the tips of the branches remain. Some shrivel and become black; others stay red, often holding a few berries somehow missed by the fall flocks of migrating birds. The panicles are so bright that from a distance they can give a reddish hue to the plant. The panicle is in the treelike shape of a raceme, the berries held on short stalks that come off a central axis. This species forms an oval cluster of berries, rather than the flat-topped clusters seen on Red Osier Dogwood and Swamp Dogwood. The plant's Latin name, *racemosa,* refers to this characteristic.

Near moist fields or open lowlands you may come across a shrub with white berries and a bright-red bark so waxy it shines like polished leather. A closer look reveals diamond-shaped lenticels and, encircling its branches, thin white lines which mark each year's growth. This plant is Red Osier Dogwood, the most striking of all Dogwood shrubs. Its color alone makes it unmistakable, but only in winter and spring; in summer, its branches tend to turn green. It is a loose, sprawling plant, with all its stems originating from the same area. The central branches sometimes grow as high as ten feet. If its panicles are still present, you will notice they are shaped like umbrellas, and any berries that remain will be white. When I encounter this plant, I can never resist gently lifting some of its lower branches to see the white roots they send down into the damp earth. These stolons, trailing branches that sprout roots where they lie along the ground, are so characteristic of Red Osier Dogwood that they are mentioned in its specific name, *stolonifera,* which means "bearing stolons." In time, new shoots grow from those points where stolons have rooted, thus continuing the vegetative reproduction of the plant.

DOGWOOD

Swamp Dogwood is aptly named, since it is one of the dominant shrubs that grow along the shady banks of streams, swamps, and lakes. You will often find it in the company of the Alder and the Buttonbush, two other water-loving shrubs. The roots of these species penetrate into the mudbanks of waterways and help prevent erosion. The U.S. Soil Conservation Service especially recommends the use of Swamp Dogwood in these areas, for in addition to preventing erosion, it provides food and cover for wildlife.

Like Red Osier Dogwood, Swamp Dogwood is a sprawling shrub, with many stems originating from one common point. Its dark-blue berries are also borne on umbrella-shaped umbels, rather than on the treelike raceme of a Gray-stemmed Dogwood. Its twigs are typically dark maroon, adding yet another subtle color to the winter landscape. If you look closely at its branch tips, you will see that they are lined with fine silky hairs, which accounts for another common name of the plant, Silky Dogwood. Swamp Dogwood has also been called Kinnikinnik, a name given to a blend of leaves and bark once smoked by certain Indian tribes of the Midwest. Among its ingredients were dried leaves of Tobacco and Bearberry and shavings from the bark of Swamp Dogwood.

A fourth species, less common than the other three, is Round-leaved

Flowers and leaf-roll on Swamp Dogwood

DOGWOOD

Dogwood. Its stems are green, unlike those of the other species, and its leaves are large and round. These plants are found mostly in dry, rocky woods. If you visit Round-leaved Dogwood in August, you will find a colorful treat, for its fruits turn a light sky blue and the stalks that hold them are a shocking pink.

Dogwoods are rated fifth among all woody plants in North America for their food value to wildlife, with only Pine, Oak, Blackberry, and Cherry more valuable. It is primarily the berries of the shrubs that are important in this respect, and each species is prolific in producing fruits. Dogwood berries are favored over the fruits of most other shrubs, which, although they mature at the same time, are left on their shrubs long after Dogwood berries have been eaten. Flocks of migrating Grackles, Robins, and Starlings descend upon the plants in fall and strip them of their fruits, eating as many as fifty berries each in one visit. Other birds that regularly consume Dogwood berries are Mockingbirds, Cardinals, Evening Grosbeaks, and Cedar Waxwings. In winter, the twigs and buds are also eaten by Ruffed Grouse, Rabbit, Chipmunk, Moose, and Deer.

In outward appearance, the flowers of Dogwood shrubs are not at all like those of the tree species. They are flat or dome-shaped clusters of creamy white blossoms, and except for the fact that each small flower has four petals instead of five, they look very much like the flower clusters of the Viburnums. Go out in May and June to find them; there are usually many clusters on each plant and although they don't have a particularly pleasant smell, they add a great deal to the beauty of the early summer landscape.

PEPPERBUSH

Clethra

ORDER: *Ericales.*   FAMILY: *Clethraceae.*   GENUS: *Clethra.*
SPECIES: *C. alnifolia,* Sweet Pepperbush;
C. acuminata, Mountain Pepperbush.

LATE ONE SUMMER while exploring near a river, I was drawn to a shrub I didn't recognize by a heavy, sweet fragrance, much like that of Lilacs. The plant had spikes of luxuriant white blossoms and shiny-surfaced leaves, and offered such a wealth of sensations that I was surprised I had never come across it before. I assumed that it was a foreign ornamental, and I drew its leaf and flowers in my notebook so that I could identify it when I got home. I was surprised to find that it was Sweet Pepperbush, a plant I had first learned of the previous winter and had come to know by its sinuate branching; smooth, dark bark; and vertical spikes of dried fruit capsules. Now that I had seen it in its summer habit, I had an intimate understanding of why the word "sweet" was included in its common name.

The flowers of Sweet Pepperbush may smell like Lilacs, but their blooming time is at the opposite end of the season. They start to blossom in July and sometimes continue even into September. The long flower spikes mature from the bottom up, a few new blossoms opening each day. At first the petals open only slightly, with just the anthers projecting, so that any insect visiting the flower is bound to get pollen on itself as it searches for nectar. As the flower matures, the petals open wider and the stamens bend out to its sides. The pistil then elongates past the anthers and becomes receptive by opening at its tip. Next, the stamens wither and fall off along with the petals, leaving only the pistil. The flower is therefore essentially proterandrous, which means that it is first male and then female. Since the spike of flowers blooms from the bottom up, the flowers at the bottom of the spike will have become female as the newly opening male flowers bloom above. This pattern corresponds perfectly with the habits of most

PEPPERBUSH

bees, which tend to land at the bottom of a spike and crawl upward. As they leave the male flowers at the top of one spike, they carry pollen to the base of the next spike, where most of the flowers are in their female stage. This strategy obviously increases the chances of cross-pollination.

An interesting aspect of Pepperbush's development is that while the flowers of its blooming spike point outward in all directions (so that the plant can provide the greatest amount of access to the visiting insects), its fruits as they mature turn upward. Their function has changed, and they are now small cups that must hold the seeds and allow them to be shaken out gradually by wind and passing animals.

One late summer day, I went out to see what insects were visiting Pepperbush flowers. Many Honeybees and Bumblebees were busily collecting nectar, and on one of the leaves I noticed what I took to be a wasp, since it had a large head, a thin waist, and black wings. As I examined it more closely, I realized it was actually a fly, for it had only one pair of wings. I made a careful drawing of it and, at home, looked it up, to discover that it had a fascinating life cycle. It belonged to the family *Conopidae,* or Big-headed Flies, many of which look like wasps. Their eggs are laid on bees; their larvae mature inside the living bee, finally killing it. In some cases, they even pupate within their host. So it was not an accident that this Big-headed Fly was visiting Sweet Pepperbush, one of the richest sources

Sweet Pepperbush

Flowers of Sweet Pepperbush

of nectar in late summer, and likely to attract many bees for the fly to parasitize.

The family *Clethraceae* has only one genus, *Clethra,* which has only two representative species in North America. The other twenty-eight or more species grow in Central America, South America, and Japan. Sweet Pepperbush is our most common species. Its specific name, *alnifolia,* means "leaves like alder"; the size, serrations, and vein patterns of the leaves of the two plants are indeed very similar. Both plants are also found in the same habitats, in moist, rich soils near still or moving water. Even Pepperbush's generic name, *Clethra,* is the Greek word for alder.

The other North American species of *Clethra,* Mountain Pepperbush, is found in an entirely different habitat. To see it, you will have to go to the Virginias, Carolinas, or Georgia, and walk up into the beautiful Appalachian and Smoky mountains. You will find the shrub in the forest, growing in rich hillside soil. Mountain Pepperbush's Latin specific name, *acuminata,* means "pointed" and refers to the pointed tips of the leaves. The flowers, fruits, and branching of this species are similar to those of Sweet Pepperbush, but its bark is very different, being brownish red and peeling off in tiny vertical shavings.

The new woody growth of Pepperbush has one very unusual trait—it is forked or branched. Though this may not seem odd, the majority of woody plants do not grow in this manner. On other trees and shrubs you will find that the most recent woody growth is unbranched; it is all straight, with no side twigs. Also, in these plants, new branches always start from buds, and

PEPPERBUSH

so have a ring of bud scale scars at their base. On Pepperbush, however, the most recent year's growth of twigs may already have side branches, and since these side branches do not start from buds, they have no ring of bud scale scars at their base. All this is far easier to see than describe, so go out in winter and examine the most recent twigs of woody plants and then those of Pepperbush, and see if you can spot the difference.

During the summer of the United States Bicentennial, I celebrated the Fourth of July by going to a favorite wild section of a nearby river and sitting in the midday sun. The Pepperbush had just started to bloom at the river's edge and over the shallows Dragonflies darted about among the flowers of the Pickerelweed. The river moved along at a slow pace, its surface absolutely smooth. I thought about when Europeans first arrived on the continent and what the river must have looked like then. I tried to take myself back in time and imagined that when I left the river I would walk into the world of 1776. It was a vivid daydream which has remained with me, and the rich smell of the Pepperbush growing naturally by the river will always be a part of my imagined journey into the untouched wilderness of the past.

Branching and seedheads
of Pepperbush in winter

RHODODENDRON, AZALEA

Rhododendron

ORDER: *Ericales.*   FAMILY: *Ericaceae.*   GENUS: *Rhododendron.*
SPECIES: *R. maximum,* Rosebay; *R. catawbiense,* Mountain Rosebay;
R. canadense, Rhodora; *R. calendulaceum,* Flame Azalea;
R. nudiflorum, Pinxter Flower; *R. viscosum,* Clammy Azalea;
R. arborescens, Smooth Azalea, and many others.

SPECIES OF *Rhododendron* are so commonly used in landscaping private homes and public places that many people are unaware that they grow naturally in our woods as well, without any trucks or shovels being used to get them there. Members of the genus, which includes both Azaleas and Rhododendrons, are best known for their exquisite flowers. Flame Azalea is one of the most famous, its bright-orange to deep-red blossoms creating the impression of fire when it is in bloom on the slopes of the southern mountains. Two other species are prized for their delicate pink blossoms, which usually open before their leaves emerge. These are the Pinxter Flower, a fairly tall shrub found in woods and at the edge of swamps, and Rhodora, a small shrub (usually less than three feet high) that grows in bogs and in acid, rocky areas and is eagerly sought out for its beauty by those who know it. In midsummer, the white-flowered species are prominent, one of the most common being Clammy Azalea or Swamp Azalea, whose flower is especially fragrant in the evening. There are only two main species of Rhododendron: Rosebay, with white flowers and a wide distribution, and Mountain Rosebay, which has rose- or lilac-colored flowers and is more limited in its range, growing primarily in the southern mountains.

Some friends once invited me over to celebrate the summer solstice and

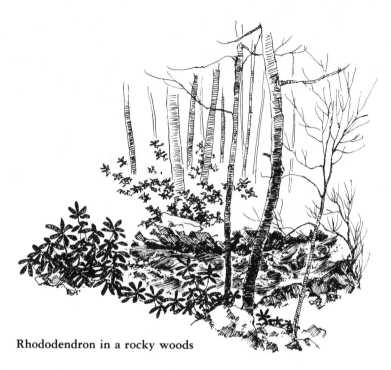

Rhododendron in a rocky woods

after a festive dinner, we all walked outside to enjoy the evening. A huge grove of Rhododendrons grew in the area, and their white blooms shone out into the deepening darkness. As we approached the plants, there was suddenly a streak of movement across our vision. We moved closer and soon someone spotted the visitor. There, in front of the Rhododendron flowers, a Sphinx moth hovered like a Hummingbird. Its wings were invisible, and its body moved gently back and forth as it probed for nectar deep within the blooms. In an instant it seemed to disappear, until we checked nearby blossoms and found that it had merely darted laterally. By the time we left the spot, it was so dark that it was hard to distinguish individual leaves, though the white flowers were still easily seen, an advertisement of which the Sphinx moths were clearly taking advantage.

All the flowers of the shrubs in the genus *Rhododendron* have basically the same arrangement for pollination, the only differences being in the color of their blossoms and in the lengths of their floral tubes. The pollinators come to the flowers for nectar, for although the blooms have pollen, it is difficult for the insects to collect. The five petals are distinct at the mouth of the flower but are joined together at their bases to form a tube. The pistil and stamens project out in front of the petals. In most species, the stamens are different lengths, their anthers outlining an oval tilted to the angle at which the pollinator must approach the flower. Each anther is composed of two adjacent cylinders, aligned like the barrels of a shotgun. The openings of the anthers all point toward the center of the oval landing area. The pistil is longer than the anthers, so that as an insect approaches the flower it is likely to be touched first. As the insect moves into the flower, it hits the anthers, which, when jostled, expel pollen out of their pores and onto the pollinator. After reaching into the blossom to get nectar, the pollinator then leaves for the next flower. As it approaches, it again touches the projecting pistil first, most likely brushing some of the pollen off from the previous flower.

The characteristic fruit of *Rhododendron* is a dry, elongated capsule with the remains of the pistil still attached to its tip. As it dries, the capsule splits into five parts, each part opening first at the tip and then curling backward. This same pattern is repeated on the tip of the pistil, which has five divisions on its surface. I find the dried fruits of this genus one of the most beautiful aspects of the plants and always look for them when out on winter walks.

The Azaleas are easily recognized in winter by their buds and branching patterns. The buds, grouped together at the ends of the twigs (a little like

Rosebay Rhododendron in flower

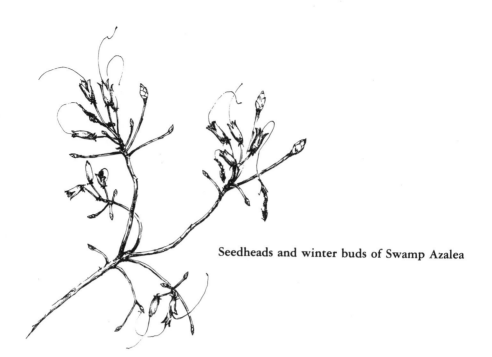

Seedheads and winter buds of Swamp Azalea

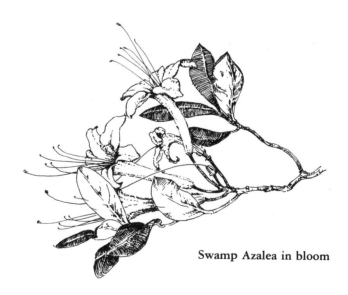

Swamp Azalea in bloom

RHODODENDRON, AZALEA

the buds of Oaks), are of two different sizes. The large ones, on the tips of the twigs, are the flower buds, and the smaller ones, just behind, are the leaf and branch buds. This arrangement is also reflected in older twig growth, where you will see fruits at the branch tips and whorls of twigs growing just beneath them. All native Azaleas are deciduous, while all our Rhododendrons are evergreen. I can usually first identify Rhododendrons in winter by their leaves, even though their bud and branching patterns are as distinctive as those of Azalea. The leaves of Rosebay Rhododendron curl up in the cold, their edges folding back and covering the undersurface of the leaf. The stomata of the leaf are located on its underside, and the curling action may protect the leaves from being dried out by winter winds. The plant also curls its foliage during times of drought. I remember as a child picking up curled leaves that had died and pretending that they were cigars.

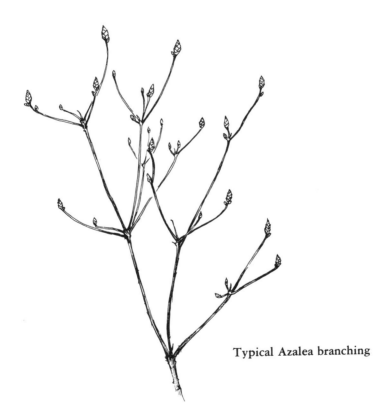

Typical Azalea branching

RHODODENDRON, AZALEA

For hundred of years, people have known about the "May apples" that appear on the twigs of Pink Azalea in late spring. The growths occur on the ends of the twigs and are about the size of a Ping-Pong ball. They look a little like the green Oak Apple Galls attached to Oak leaves in spring, but instead of being stringy and tough, they are crisp, juicy, and sweet. Further, they are not formed by an insect but rather by a bacteria or fungus, and can be eaten without harm to the plant or to yourself. They were more well known in colonial times and were even pickled and stored for later eating. These galls are not to be confused with the edible (only when fully ripe) fruit from May Apple, a low herbaceous plant with the scientific name *Podophyllum peltatum.*

In general, the species of *Rhododendron* do not have much value for wildlife. The only significant exception is the Rhododendrons, whose evergreen leaves are browsed during winter by the White-tailed Deer when more favorable plants have all been eaten. The leaves of Rhododendrons have been reported to be detrimental to livestock if eaten in large quantities, but the Deer do not seem to be affected. (The same holds true for Laurels, which are poisonous to livestock if consumed to any great extent, but which the wild Deer feed on in limited amounts.)

Azaleas hybridize freely, even in the wild, and so there are many regional varieties which are mixtures of the characteristics of more widespread species. Horticulturists have taken advantage of this ability and produced what seem to be endless variations by mixing Azaleas in North America with those of Japan and China. Many of our most important hybrids contain strains from plants of the Himalayas, where in certain areas of the mountainsides Rhododendrons are the dominant plants.

LAUREL

Kalmia

ORDER: *Ericales.*   FAMILY: *Ericaceae.*   GENUS: *Kalmia.*
SPECIES: *K. latifolia,* Mountain Laurel;
K. angustifolia, Sheep Laurel; *K. polifolia,* Pale Laurel,
and others.

THE GENUS NAME of the Laurels, *Kalmia,* refers to a Swedish botanist, Pehr Kalm, a pupil of Linnaeus, who came to America in the mid eighteenth century. He wandered over the eastern part of the continent in search of interesting plants, and collected the new species that he found to bring back to his teacher. On his return to Europe, he gave over six hundred specimens to Linnaeus to aid in the master's work on classification. Linnaeus wanted to reward his pupil's careful discoveries and so named the Laurels, one of Kalm's favorite plants, in his honor.

Laurels are well-known shrubs, used widely in landscape planting; their evergreen leaves are also familiar from Christmas decorations. There are three main species of the plant in eastern North America. Mountain Laurel is the largest and usually appears as a shrub five to ten feet high, although in the south it occasionally may grow to thirty feet tall and look more like a tree. This plant seems to thrive in rocky, acidic soil and often develops into dense stands that fill the understory of Oak and other hardwood forests. The stands are a result of two means of vegetative reproduction: a spreading root system that grows new shoots, and "layering," in which branches that touch the ground grow roots at their points of contact with the earth.

The other two species of Laurel, Sheep Laurel and Pale Laurel, are small, thin shrubs usually no more than two or three feet tall. Sheep Laurel is the more common, being found in a variety of habitats, from the edges of dry fields to the moist ground surrounding swamps and boggy areas. Pale

Mountain Laurel in
snow-filled woods

Laurel is much more restricted in its environment, growing only in boglike conditions. These two species can be easily distinguished by the placement of their flowers and fruits: Pale Laurel bears both on the tips of its branches, while Sheep Laurel bears them laterally off the sides of the past year's growth. Our common Laurel species all bloom in early summer. Mountain Laurel flowers are the most showy because the plants are large and produce dense clusters of white blossoms that stand out against the plants' dark evergreen leaves. The smaller flowers of the shorter Sheep and Pale Laurel are less conspicuous, but their spectacular deep-pink color and finely tooled form make them even more rewarding to find. But this genus's flowers are remarkable not only for their beauty but also for their ingenious pollination mechanism. Every Laurel bloom is composed of five petals fused together into a shallow dish; in each of the petals are two small indentations. Ten stamens project from the center of the flower, their anthers lodged into the indentations of the petals and their filaments bent and under tension. They are like ten tiny catapults, all set to spring upon the first insect visitor. A single pistil rests among the bases of the stamens and projects out in front of the flower.

The most common pollinators of the Laurels are usually Bumblebees or Honeybees. As they arrive and try to land in the floral cup, they very likely

Sheep Laurel leaves and fruits

first hit the pistil, which stands in their landing path. In doing so, they rub off some of the pollen that they accumulated from visiting other Laurel blooms. Once in the center of the flower, the insect begins to probe for nectar at the base of the stamens, moving them sufficiently for their tips to be freed from the pockets in the petals and spring up. Their anthers, shaped like two small cups, shower their pollen on the insect. In the case of Mountain Laurel, the pollen grains are connected by sticky strands that assure their being carried on the insect to the next flower. Because the flowers of the genus advertise no pollen (since it is all hidden in the petals), their insect visitors are most likely seeking only nectar.

By fall, Laurel flowers have matured into small, five-part capsules. If you break one apart, you will find what appears to be only fine brown dust. This "dust" is in fact the plant's seeds, which are so minute that a single capsule

Flowers of Mountain Laurel

LAUREL

(which is about half the size of a pea) may contain five to seven hundred of them. The dissemination mechanism of this seedhead is similar to that of many other shrubs in the family *Ericaceae:* its sides split open along five small slits and the seeds are blown out and dispersed by the wind. The seeds remain living through the winter and germinate the following spring. Patches of low moss seem to be particularly favorable for germination, possibly because the moss creates ideal moisture conditions for the seed-lings.

In winter, look for white-fringed black dots on the undersides of Laurel leaves, particularly those of Mountain Laurel. These dots are formed by scale insects, or *Coccidae.* The female of the species excretes a waxy shell and leaves her eggs beneath it to overwinter. The small scales are a fascinating sight, and through a magnifying glass their delicately fringed edges show up more clearly. Chickadees and Kinglets feed on these eggs throughout the winter.

The benefit of Laurels to wildlife is due primarily to the cover they provide when growing in dense stands. Their food value is limited, since their fruits are dry and minute and their leaves and stems contain chemicals that are toxic to at least some animals. Although Deer are known to feed on the evergreen leaves in winter, especially in the south, and don't seem to suffer any ill effects, livestock that eat the leaves usually become sick and sometimes die. This toxicity accounts for the other common name of Sheep Laurel—Lambkill.

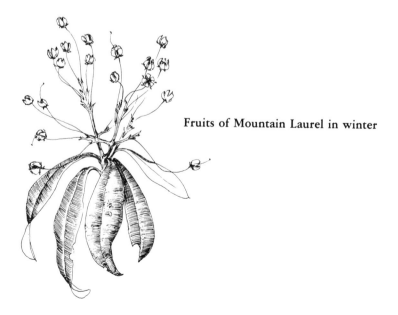

Fruits of Mountain Laurel in winter

LYONIA

Lyonia

ORDER: *Ericales.*   FAMILY: *Ericaceae.*   GENUS: *Lyonia.*
SPECIES: *L. lucida,* Fetterbush; *L. mariana,* Staggerbush;
L. ligustrina, Maleberry.

THE GENUS NAME *Lyonia* was given to this group of plants by the famous American naturalist Thomas Nuttall, in honor of John Lyon, an early American botanist who hunted for new plants in the southern Appalachian Mountains. He researched many medicinal cures made with native plants and in 1803 reported seeing several specimens of *Franklinia* trees. If he did actually locate some of these trees, then he was one of the last people to do so, for they have never been seen in the wild since. From the journals of John Lyon, it does not seem that he was particularly interested in the natural history of plants, but rather in making large collections for commercial purposes. He often gathered hundreds of samples of the same species from a single area, and although this practice was probably questionable even in those days, it would be unthinkable now, when such actions could easily endanger the survival of a species.

The most widespread species of *Lyonia* in eastern North America is called Maleberry, and to this day I have no clue to the reason behind the common name. The scientific name, *ligustrina,* means that the plant resembles plants in the genus *Ligustrum,* or Privet. It is true that the leaves of both species are lanceolate and about the same size, but all resemblance ends here, and so even the Latin name is obscure. Maleberry's flowers are small, almost spherical bells. They are about half the size of those of most other ericaceous shrubs with the same type of flower, and one wonders if they attract a special, smaller species of pollinator. Maleberry has a tendency to grow near swamps and boggy areas. If you visit these places in winter, look for the shrub's small bright-red buds along the tips of its twigs.

Maleberry fruits
and winter twigs

    Staggerbush is another wide-ranging species of *Lyonia,* growing from the Gulf Coast all the way up to the southern portions of New England. Its flowers are about ten times as large as those of Maleberry, and interestingly, they are just about the largest of this bell-type flower within the Ericads. Staggerbush generally grows in drier, sandy soil or in lowland peaty areas.

    While Staggerbush and Maleberry are both deciduous plants, the third eastern species of *Lyonia* is evergreen. It is commonly called Fetterbush, even though this same common name is given to *Pieris floribunda.* Fetterbush grows only in the far south and in habitats similar to those of Staggerbush. Its flowers are midway in size between those of the other two eastern species and are sometimes slightly pink or even red. Fetterbush's scientific name, *lucida,* undoubtedly refers to its "shining" evergreen leaves, which have the distinguishing trait of two veins that run adjacent and parallel to either margin of the leaf.

LYONIA

A great many of the plants in the family *Ericaceae* have very similar characteristics. Blueberry, Huckleberry, Leatherleaf, Bog Rosemary, Andromeda, Leucothoe, and Lyonia all have little white bell-like flowers. And in each of them, the pollination mechanism is basically the same. Their anthers, double-barreled tubes with openings at their tips, are arranged around a single style in such a way that the pollen cannot fall out. The flower hangs vertically, so that when an insect probes for nectar, the anthers are moved away from the style and the pollen falls down upon the pollinator's face.

Many of the Ericads have the same basic structure to their fruits as well. Andromeda, Laurel, Leatherleaf, Leucothoe, Bog Rosemary, and Lyonia all produce clusters of dried capsules that split into five parts and release fine seeds into the air as the wind blows across them. These plants are also woody shrubs, and most of them are found growing in acidic soils. They all have roughly lanceolate leaves which in many cases are tough and leathery and often evergreen. Every one of these characteristics can be found in plants within the genus *Lyonia.*

Besides sharing many traits, the Ericads have diverged in important ways as well. One of the most interesting of these divergences is the timing of

Maleberry flowers

the growth cycle from a bud to a matured fruit. In one study, it was discovered that there are basically three different timings of this growth among genera of *Ericaceae*. One type of growth takes only a single growing season and is completed before the winter sets in. In this pattern, a leafy shoot grows from a bud in spring and flower buds are produced on it by early summer. In midsummer, the flowers bloom, and by late fall they have ripened into fruits. This is a pattern typical of many of our shrubs; in the *Ericaceae*, it is represented by Sourwood, *Oxydendrum arboreum*, one of the few members of this family that is a tree.

Another type of growth is represented by Leatherleaf, *Chamaedaphne calyculata*. A leafy shoot sprouts in early summer, and by mid to late summer, flower buds have developed and have even matured their pollen and other sexual parts. Although they are ready to bloom, they remain in this stage through fall and winter, blossoming early the next spring and maturing seeds by summer. This plant therefore requires one and a half growing seasons to complete its cycle. Shrubs with this type of growth are always the really early bloomers, and often they flower before their leaves have emerged. Members of the genus *Leucothoe* also have this pattern of growth.

A third style of growth is represented by *Lyonia* and Bog Rosemary, *Andromeda glaucophylla*. These plants, too, produce leafy shoots in spring, and follow with early development of flower buds in midsummer. But instead of maturing before winter, the flower buds remain immature and overwinter in that state. They finish their development the next spring, bloom in summer, and mature seeds by the fall. This method of development is the slowest, needing two full growing seasons to complete the cycle from bud to matured fruit. It is fascinating to speculate on the advantages of each of these three strategies. Some of the factors involved may be: availability of nutrients in the environment, optimal times for seed dispersal, and competition for pollinators at the time of blooming.

LEUCOTHOE

Leucothoe

ORDER: *Ericales.*   FAMILY: *Ericaceae.*   GENUS: *Leucothoe.*
SPECIES: *L. axillaris,* Downy Leucothoe;
L. editorum, Drooping Leucothoe; *L. recurva,* Mountain Leucothoe;
L. racemosa, Swamp Leucothoe.

THE LEUCOTHOES are divided into two basic groups, which differ greatly in appearance. One group, which typically grows in southern deciduous forests, contains Drooping Leucothoe and Downy Leucothoe. These are both low, sprawling shrubs with shiny evergreen leaves and are often found growing in the same areas as Laurels and Rhododendrons. Their branches, which frequently remain green all year, sometimes root at their tips where they touch the ground. This ability enables the plant to create dense thickets that are difficult to walk through, accounting for the common name Dog Hobble which is given to either of these species. A similar mode of growth and the word "hobble" also apply to *Viburnum alnifolium,* Hobblebush.

The members of the other group of Leucothoes, Mountain Leucothoe and Swamp Leucothoe, are less well known, and have very few distinctive traits. They are tall, upright shrubs with small deciduous leaves and are found either in small groups or as single plants. They often grow with Highbush Blueberry or Lyonia, and at various times of year can be easily mistaken for either.

One characteristic shared by the two groups of Leucothoe is their tiny white bell-shaped flowers. These bloom in spring, are quite fragrant, and are borne in clusters off small branches. The flowers have the same pollination strategy as many other ericaceous plants (described in the section on Huckleberry). The name Leucothoe refers to a Babylonian princess whom Apollo transformed into a sweet-smelling plant.

Drooping Leucothoe in winter

In late summer, look at the branches of Swamp Leucothoe and you will see new growth of slim twigs covered with small, swollen red buds. When I first encountered these twigs, I concluded that the plants had not yet bloomed that year; I was wrong, however, for its flowers had opened in early spring, and what I was seeing were in fact the preformed flowers of the following year. As was explained in the Lyonia section, three different modes of growth can be distinguished in the *Ericaceae,* each of which requires a different amount of time for the flowering shoot to mature into a fruit. Leucothoe, which takes one and a half growing seasons to complete the process, falls into the middle category. A flowering shoot is produced in spring; by fall, the flowers are fully matured in the bud state and have even produced pollen and ovules, but they remain dormant, to bloom early the next spring and mature fruits by midsummer. This blooming sequence also applies to the other deciduous species of Leucothoe, Mountain Leucothoe. The two evergreen species have a somewhat different cycle: although they overwinter with long and catkin-like flower buds, they do not produce pollen until the following spring.

LEUCOTHOE

The fruit cases of all species of Leucothoe are small, woody capsules; the seeds they contain look much like brown dust and are scattered by the wind. The remains of the style of the pistil typically project from the dried seedheads. Leucothoe provides very little food for wildlife, except as browse for Deer. As is true of some other ericaceous shrubs, its leaves are reported to be poisonous to livestock. The evergreen species are probably most valuable, since they provide dense cover for birds and mammals in winter.

Since the genus *Leucothoe* contains both evergreen and deciduous species, it provides an interesting case study for an examination of the differences in these two strategies of leaf growth. A general trend among plants in the East is that if there are both evergreen and deciduous species in the same genus, the deciduous species tend to range farther north. This is true of Leucothoe, Oaks, Hollies, Rhododendrons and Azaleas, Bayberries, Blueberries and Cranberries, Honeysuckles, and Greenbriers. In northern areas, the extended cold season is like a period of drought. The available water is locked up in ice, and the ground is often frozen. Since leaves are the main parts of plants that release water, those plants that keep their leaves through winter drought run the risk of dying from desiccation. Therefore, most plants that grow in areas of extreme cold shed their leaves

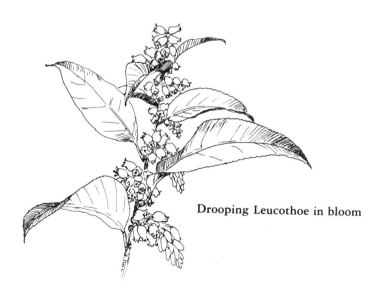

Drooping Leucothoe in bloom

before the ground freezes, and for even more protection, seal over the areas where leaves were attached to their stems.

Another interesting distinction between the evergreen and deciduous species of Leucothoe is in the leaves themselves. The deciduous species have thin, papery, and dull-surfaced leaves, while the evergreen species have thick, leathery leaves covered with a waxy coating, which is especially thick on their upper surface. These differences are typical for all deciduous and evergreen leaves.

Both strategies of leaf growth involve compromises. The deciduous plant has leaves perfectly suited for the rapid exchange of gases needed during the hot summer months, but it also must produce an entire set of new leaves each year. The evergreen plant can use its leaves for more than one season, but to last through winter, they must also be thick and have a waxy covering, requirements that cut down on their efficiency during the summer growing period.

LEATHERLEAF
Chamaedaphne

ORDER: *Ericales.* FAMILY: *Ericaceae.* GENUS: *Chamaedaphne.*
SPECIES: *C. calyculata,* Leatherleaf.

LEATHERLEAF IS a plant common in all the colder regions of the Northern Hemisphere. It is a delicate little shrub, usually only two to three feet high, and most often found with its roots in water and its thin, arched stems lined with a progression of increasingly smaller evergreen leaves. One of its most charming features is that it is always in the company of certain other plants. This habit can be explained by the fact that Leatherleaf and its companions grow only in very specific conditions—conditions typical of northern bogs. In such an environment, Leatherleaf is often the dominant plant and plays an important role in bog succession, the long-term change in the kinds of species that are present in these areas. Leatherleaf may also be found at the edges of lakes, in small coves, or in the backwaters of cold, slow-moving streams, all small areas that have developed boglike conditions.

There are many definitions of a bog and many opinions on how a bog differs from a swamp. In general, a bog is a combination of physical characteristics and vegetation type. The most important physical characteristic is the presence of fairly cold, noncirculating acidic water that is generally light brown, and poor in minerals, potassium, and nitrogen. The vegetation characteristics are: a mat of plants growing in the water without attachment to the ground, a great number of species from the family *Ericaceae,* Sphagnum Moss, and a buildup of peat at the bottom of the water and among the floating mats of plants.

Bogs typically follow a unique pattern of succession, in which Leatherleaf plays an important role. The creation of a bog starts in small areas of still

Leatherleaf in winter

water. In these sites, plants begin to grow in two zones—out in the open water and along the water's edge. The first plants to grow in the open water are usually the Pondweeds, of the genus *Potamogeton.* These plants root on the bottom of the deeper water, and their leaves and flexible stems float up to just below the surface. Succeeding these underwater plants are floating-leaved species of the Waterlily family, *Nymphaeaceae,* such as Spatter-dock or Fragrant Waterlily. The first vegetation to grow along the shore will be one or more species of Sedge or *Carex; Carex lasiocarpa,* which builds a mat of interlocking roots, is especially conducive to bog development. If growing in a small protected area, this mat may extend out into the water and even crowd out the Waterlilies. It may also be prevented from growing too far beyond the shore by wave action or the breakup of ice in spring, in which case it is just a narrow band around the shoreline. Sphagnum Moss often invades the Sedges and grows out into the mat with them.

In the next stage of bog formation, various plants that grow in drier soil (typically Iris, Joe-Pye Weed, Goldenrod, and Beggar's Ticks) move in

§ 194 §

LEATHERLEAF

behind the Sedges. These are then replaced by the first shrubs in the succession, which include Leatherleaf, Bog Rosemary, and Cranberry. Leatherleaf, by far the most dominant member of this group, grows out over the mat by extending its roots into the Sphagnum and Sedges and producing new stems. The plant is dependent on the Sedges for support and buoyancy in the water. Large, dense groves of Leatherleaf are a common sight in most bogs.

After Leatherleaf has established itself, other shrubs and trees follow, including Bog Willow, Mountain Holly, Alder, Swamp Birch, Swamp Dogwood, Winterberry Holly, Larch, Spruce, and Cedar. These plants all grow taller than Leatherleaf and eventually create so much shade that the stands of Leatherleaf become less vigorous and gradually die. However, for

Leatherleaf branching pattern

all forms of succession, a tidy written description rarely mirrors any given example in nature. So just keep in mind the general pattern and expect to see only variations of it in the wild.

I used to think that Leatherleaf's manner of growth involved producing each year just a new branch that bent so that it became horizontal at its tip. Along this branch would be arranged progressively smaller leaves. But I had not looked closely enough; the plant actually grows two types of branches and two types of leaves. Each summer, the first growth is the main vegetative vertical branch with large leaves; sprouting horizontally off this is a smaller twig, with flower buds and smaller leaves. The two forms of branch, with their respective leaves, can be seen throughout fall and winter. In the following year, once the flowers have bloomed and the seeds matured, the small horizontal twig sheds its leaves and dies, while the vertical branch to which it was attached remains alive and keeps its leaves for another year or two. It continues its growth, again forming a new section of vertical stem with a horizontal twig at its tip.

It has been discovered that in very cold areas, the number of successful blooms on Leatherleaf in the spring depends to a great extent on the height of the snow during the previous winter. When the plants are totally exposed to the cold and drying winds, then only one or two flower buds, nearest the main stem, mature into flowers. If, except for the top branches, the plant is well covered by snow, then about 30 percent of the flowers mature. If the entire plant is covered with snow, then almost all the flowers bloom.

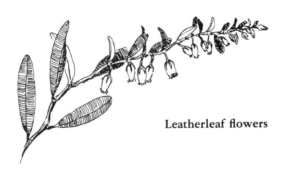

Leatherleaf flowers

LEATHERLEAF

The bell-like flower of Leatherleaf is similar to that of many closely related plants, such as Blueberry, Lyonia, Pieris, Bog Rosemary, and Leucothoe. It points downward, forcing a visiting insect to grasp the upward curving tips of the petals or the top of the bloom as it probes inside the corolla for nectar. When entering the flower, the insect first brushes against its protruding pistil. Inside the blossom, the stamens have double-barreled anthers with small pores at their tips. These pores are pressed against the central pistil; as the insect's mouth touches them, the pore openings are moved away from the pistil and the pollen falls out onto the insect's face. This pollen will then rub off on the pistil of the next flower that is visited.

After the flower is pollinated, the small white corolla and the anthers that were attached to it fall off, but the pistil remains as a small projecting needle that can be seen even after the fruits have matured. The ripened fruits point upward, in contrast to the pendulous flowers. They form a type of "rattlebox" common to many plants—a small cup split at the seams which holds the seeds until they are jostled out by the action of raindrops, wind, or passing animals.

HUCKLEBERRY

Gaylussacia

ORDER: *Ericales.*   FAMILY: *Ericaceae.*   GENUS: *Gaylussacia.*
SPECIES: *G. dumosa,* Dwarf Huckleberry;
G. frondosa, Blue Huckleberry; *G. baccata,* Black Huckleberry,
and many others.

LIKE MANY PEOPLE, I had always assumed that Huckleberry was another common name for Blueberry. I had heard the name mentioned frequently, but never imagined that it was a distinct plant that I might find or a fruit that I could gather. Some people will tell you that it is so difficult to tell Huckleberries from Blueberries that it is not worth the effort, but I have to disagree. Not only is it easy to differentiate the plants, but in my opinion it is well worth it, since I prefer eating Huckleberries—their fruits are juicier and more refreshing, and I like the crunchy seeds inside. Also, as a friend of mine is fond of pointing out, when you discover that an area contains two kinds of plants where you thought there was only one, then that spot becomes twice as interesting.

There are many ways to distinguish between Huckleberry and Blueberry. One that is a lot of fun was shown to me by a naturalist friend who picked a leaf from a Huckleberry plant and pressed its undersurface onto the back of my hand. After I peeled off the leaf, a bright-yellow mark remained on my skin. I was delighted and the experience stuck fast in my memory, as I am sure it will in yours if you try it. The spot of color is left by resin dots on the undersurface of the leaves; Blueberry leaves have no dots. The trick works best in spring and early summer, for later the surface resin dries up. The dots can even help you to identify species: all of our three common species of Huckleberry have resinous undersurfaces to their leaves, but only Black Huckleberry, our most common short species, has resin dots on top of the leaf as well. There is something special about the

HUCKLEBERRY

yellow mark; it is like a stamp you get on your hand when you enter a fairground, only this stamp signifies your membership in the group that knows Huckleberry.

Actually, I always recognize Huckleberry by its beautifully uniform dark bark, smooth right down to the base of the main stem. Only the newest twigs are of a different quality. They are a rich red, especially in winter. Blueberry, in contrast, has new twigs that are either green and red or only green; its bark is fissured and split as early as the second or third year of growth.

After learning to recognize Huckleberry, you will soon discover how common it is. Often an entire forest floor will be covered with just Black Huckleberry. Like many other shrubs, this plant regularly grows to quite distinct heights, so distinct that they can be recognized on this basis alone. Black Huckleberry, for instance, forms a shrub layer about two feet high. In the same areas you may see similar dense growth only about one foot high; this is very likely Lowbush Blueberry. Looking farther in the same spot, you may see clumps of plants about three or four feet high: in the northern woods, these will usually be Maple-leaved Viburnum. It is rewarding to come to know the plants in this way, since at the same time you acquire a sense of the layering of leafy crowns in the forest understory.

Huckleberry fruits

HUCKLEBERRY

There are two common species of the genus *Gaylussacia:* Black Huckleberry and Blue Huckleberry. Black Huckleberry grows in dense clones, spreading by underground rootstocks. In sunny open areas where these clones are well established, they tend to prevent other species of shrubs and trees from invading for many years. Blue Huckleberry is named for the powdery bloom on its berries that makes them look blue. This shrub is a tall plant about the size of Highbush Blueberry; I usually find it in small clusters, and only rarely in crowded groves. Because its berries and flowers hang off the plant on long, spindly racemes, it is often called Dangleberry. A third, less common species of *Gaylussacia* is Dwarf Huckleberry; unlike the other Huckleberries, which prefer dry soils, this plant is found in wet areas, especially in the north, where it grows chiefly in and around bogs.

The Huckleberry flower is similar to those of many other members of the family *Ericaceae.* It is basically a hanging bell, with ten stamens tipped by tubular anthers that have pores at their ends. These pores are positioned

Huckleberry branching in winter

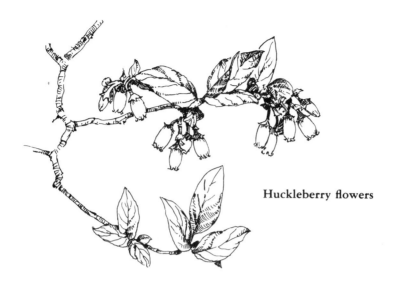

Huckleberry flowers

against the longer, centrally placed pistil so that when an insect probes for nectar, it moves the anthers away from the pistil and the pollen falls on its face. The flowers are white to pink and bloom in late spring. They are visited by various bees as well as by some of the smaller butterflies.

The fruit of Huckleberry is quite distinct from that of Blueberry. Each Blueberry contains hundreds of tiny seeds, so small that we are seldom aware of them. Each Huckleberry contains just ten seeds, which are larger and even crackle in your mouth as you chew the fruit. The fruit of Huckleberry is actually a many-seeded drupe. Like Blueberries, the Huckleberry fruits develop behind the flower's calyx, so that when mature, they are tipped by the remains of the calyx's five lobes. Huckleberries are generally not as productive as Blueberries and the fruits that are produced are only occasionally eaten by birds. This is fine with me, for it means that there are always plenty for my own trailside stops when I come across a group of the plants. If you gather the fruits soon after they ripen, you will taste them at their best; later in summer, they lose their thirst-quenching juiciness.

BLUEBERRY

Vaccinium

ORDER: *Ericales.*   FAMILY: *Ericaceae.*   GENUS: *Vaccinium.*
SPECIES: *V. vacillans,* Early Lowbush Blueberry;
V. angustifolium, Late Lowbush Blueberry;
V. corymbosum, Common Highbush Blueberry;
V. atrococcum, Black Highbush Blueberry, and many others.

BLUEBERRIES ARE easy to recognize at any time of year, especially if you look closely at their twigs. In summer, the young twigs are all green; in winter, they are red on the upper surface and green on the underside. The twigs are very fine and tend to zigzag. In just a few years, their bark will become fissured and brown, appearing much older than it really is. There are numerous species of Blueberries—some quite local, and others more widespread. The identification of species is difficult since many hybridize; therefore, I am usually satisfied with the rough division of the genus into the Highbush and Lowbush varieties.

It is often worthwhile to think about what feature of a plant we choose to use in its common name. For instance, Blueberry could just as well be called White Flower, Bell Flower, Gall Bush, or Green Twig. But that we do call it Blueberry suggests what we consider to be the most important aspect of the plant to our lives. There is nothing quite like a big bowl of fresh blueberries topped with a little cream and sugar. And of course, their use in pies, tarts, doughnuts, pancakes, jams, and jellies is well known to young and old alike. Each blueberry actually contains hundreds of seeds, but they are so minute that they never interfere with our enjoyment of the fruits.

Wildlife likes Blueberries as much as we do, especially the songbirds and certain gamebirds. Among mammals, it is the Black Bear that eats the most fruits. While canoeing in Maine, I have seen large Black Bears sitting on their haunches and feeding off Highbush Blueberries. For some reason, this sight dampens my own enthusiasm for getting out of the canoe and collecting along the shores myself. In the northeast, the twigs and leaves are eaten to a significant extent by the White-tailed Deer.

There are a number of signs of insect activity to observe on Blueberry bushes in winter. On some of the twigs you are likely to find little gray or leathery brown swellings riddled with holes. These are Blueberry Stem Galls, caused by a small wasp called *Hemadas nubilipennis.* The adult wasp lays its eggs in early summer on the new growth of the plants, and the young larvae soon eat down to just under the new green bark. Either through their action itself or through some secretion, they cause the plant to grow a swelling on one side of the twig, which usually results in the twig's bending at a 90-degree angle. At first green, the gall later turns a nice red-brown in late summer and remains this color through the winter. If you open the gall in winter, you will find ten to twenty small white wasp larvae inside. In spring, these larvae will eat their way to the edge of the gall, pupate, and leave as adults. The gall then turns gray and cracks slightly, but remains on the plant for a few more years. Two types of flies also hatch from these galls. It is believed that they are guests or inquilines,

Box of Blueberries

Blueberry Stem Galls

a term which refers to an animal that habitually lives in the nest or home of some other species. Although the flies did not form the gall, they share it and do not harm the gall-maker. Blueberries are so typically infested with this gall that seeing one of them can be a good way of recognizing the plant.

Also on the winter twigs you will see two types of buds. One is very small and pointed, while the other is much larger and is usually located nearer the twig's tip. New leaves will grow from the small buds the following spring; the larger ones will produce both leaves and flowers.

In spring, before Highbush Blueberry bushes have leaves or blooms, these plants are a good spot to find one of the most spectacular feats of engineering in the natural world. Go out in the early morning when the light is low and some dew has fallen during the night, and you will have your best chance at a sighting. What you are looking for is the web of the tiny Bowl-and-Doily Spider. It will look like either a small circus net, the kind that is suspended under aerial acrobats, or a gossamer bowl about five inches in diameter. Above the bowl will be a maze of haphazard threads, and below, a flat platform of webbing, the so-called doily. Look carefully at the structure of the bowl: it is one of the more obvious treasures of the spider world. The spider lives between the doily and the bowl. Insects hit the threads above the bowl and drop down; the spider then pulls them into the webbing of the bowl, injects a paralyzing liquid, and stores them for later eating.

The flowers of all Blueberries bloom in late spring or early summer, and a few species will even continue to bloom through June. The flowers are borne in clusters and their pollination mechanism is like that of many other Ericaceous shrubs. Once, while watching some Bumblebees collecting nectar from a Highbush Blueberry, I witnessed a fascinating incident. I was trying to see how pollination actually occurred, when I noticed that many of the bees were landing at the base of the flowers, remaining for a short time, and then flying on. They were not hanging off the bottom of the petals, as they would have had to if the pollination mechanism were to work. I examined some of the flowers after a bee had left them and found

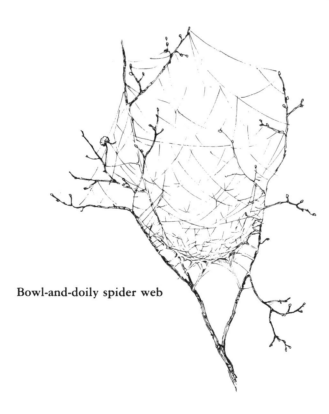

Bowl-and-doily spider web

BLUEBERRY

that each had a small brown hole that punctured its petals. Suddenly a bee landed on a flower cluster right in front of me and I had a chance to see exactly what it did. It paused at each flower, stuck its mouthparts through the base of the petals, and sucked out some of the nectar. I was shocked. These bees were taking nectar from Blueberry flowers without pollinating them. Nature was not working properly. How could this be?

After my initial surprise, I began to think more clearly about what I had seen. My impression that nature was malfunctioning was due to my lapsing into the belief that I was seeing the end result of evolution. This battle of adaptations between the bee and the flower is the result of evolution, but not the end of it. Evolution keeps happening—you are always in the middle of it. This is important to remember when looking at any life, whether it is Blueberry flowers or ourselves.

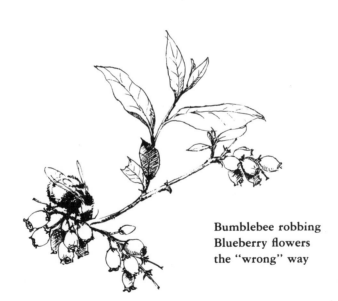

Bumblebee robbing
Blueberry flowers
the "wrong" way

NIGHTSHADE

Solanum

ORDER: *Tubiflorae.*   FAMILY: *Solanaceae.*   GENUS: *Solanum.*
SPECIES: *S. Dulcamara,* Nightshade; *S. nigrum,* Black Nightshade.

"CLAMBERING" IS defined as "climbing with both hands and feet." This is a perfect description of what Nightshade does, for it uses neither tendrils (like Grapes) nor disks (like Virginia Creeper), nor does it really twine (like Bittersweet), although it seems to try. More often it is found just falling loosely over anything and in any way it can to support itself in the sunlight, and a fairly sloppy appearance is generally the result.

A number of features of Nightshade may remind you of certain parts of plants that you have seen in your vegetable garden. For instance, its flowers look a lot like those of Eggplant, and with some imagination, the fruits look like miniature Eggplants. The leaves of Nightshade resemble those of your young Tomato plants. There is good reason for this similarity—all these plants are in the same family, *Solanaceae,* which also includes the Peppers and Potatoes. Most of these food plants, introduced to Europe from South America or India, were eyed with great caution because they were related to Belladonna (or Deadly Nightshade), *Atropa belladonna,* which was well known in Europe as a powerful poison. Tomatoes and Eggplants were first used only as ornamentals until public opinion was swayed and the plants were considered to be edible.

Nightshade has some distinctive features in winter. The vine's old leaf scars are raised and quite rounded, and just above them you are likely to see the new leaf buds. If you look just below each leaf bud, you will see a lovely flattened portion that gives the stem an attractive five-angled appearance at these points. The old seed stalks, often conspicuous on the winter vine, are one of the best ways to identify the plant in this season, if none of its fruits are left. The seed stalk has numerous branches, each of which is tipped with the five-parted calyx that remains after the fruit has fallen.

The flower of Nightshade is misleading: with its five dark-purple petals setting off a bright yellow center, it looks as if it were advertising the presence of pollen to passing insects. But if you touch the yellow anthers, you will find that no pollen rubs off on your fingers. The strategy of this flower is one of deception: it attracts insects on the pretense that there is food to gather, while in fact it secretes no nectar and what looks like pollen is just the yellow color of the anthers. The anthers are fused together into a cone around the pistil, and the actual pollen is discharged through openings at their tips. As the visiting insect lands on the cone of anthers, grasping it tightly, pollen is blown out the anther tips onto its abdomen. The insect then carries this pollen to the next flower, where some rubs off on the projecting pistil. There are both advantages and disadvantages to deception as a pollination strategy. An advantage is that the plant does not have to produce food for the insects and so conserves energy. The disadvantage is that insects will not keep returning to the flowers, for once they have tested a few blooms and find no food, they will leave. To put it in the vernacular, Nightshade is dependent on a sucker being born every minute.

Whether self-pollinated or insect-pollinated, Nightshade has a high per-

Nightshade flowers

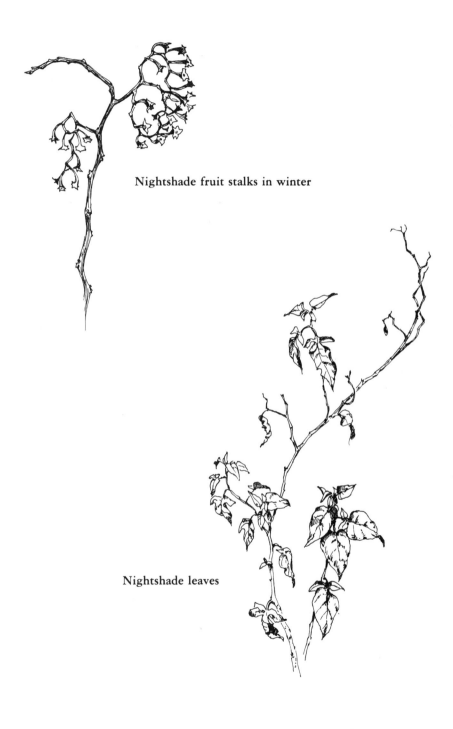

Nightshade fruit stalks in winter

Nightshade leaves

centage of flowers that mature into fruits. The fruits are berries which turn from green to yellow to shiny red. They seem to ripen at different rates, so the berries on any given fruit cluster are always colorful. Their beauty should not be taken as an invitation to eat them or even taste them, for they are reported to be very bitter and in a few cases may be poisonous. There is some question as to how toxic the various members of the Nightshade genus are, but it is definitely known that our native species are all at least extremely unpalatable. Nightshade and Black Nightshade (a similar plant, but with white-petaled flowers and black fruits) are both native to Europe and introduced into North America; Black Nightshade's fruits are known to be very poisonous when immature. Nightshade has spread rapidly since its introduction, mainly because so many birds feed on the berries and then pass the seeds through in their droppings. Thirty-one birds are known to consume the fruits, and twelve species of mammals use the fruits or leaves as food.

Nightshade leaves vary in shape, some being lobed and others entire. In fall, they turn a beautiful shade of dark purple, a color unlike that in any of our other shrubs or vines. Forming a background to the red of the fruits, this coloring makes fall one of Nightshade's most spectacular seasons.

Nightshade fruits

TRUMPET VINE

Campsis

ORDER: *Tubiflorae.*　　FAMILY: *Bignoniaceae.*　　GENUS: *Campsis.*
SPECIES: *C. radicans,* Trumpet Vine.

ALTHOUGH TRUMPET VINE is a common wild vine in the southern half
of the continent, people throughout our country like to plant it near their
homes and over arbors because of the lovely shade it creates and its flowers,
which continue to bloom for many months. It climbs up over supporting
objects, such as other plants or walls, in much the same way as Poison Ivy,
using aerial rootlets that grow directly out of the new shoots. These rootlets
are often located at the leaf nodes. The large and pinnately compound
leaves of the plant are a little like those of Elderberry—they grow in pairs
off the stems, and have a groove along the upper surface of their petiole.
Leaves are produced primarily from the most recent two years of growth;
at that point, the stems become woody and no longer yield foliage. The
trunks of old vines can grow to six inches or more in diameter and their
deeply fissured bark gnarls with age.

　　Trumpet Vine is a joyous sight when in bloom, its large, trumpet-like
flowers sounding forth their triumphant blasts of red color, never nodding
but always horizontal and self-proclaiming. Flowers are proclaimers in most
plants and Trumpet Vine's proclamation is intended especially for the eyes
and habits of the Ruby-throated Hummingbird. Worldwide, birds are important pollinators of plants: over sixteen hundred species are adapted to
feeding on nectar. The vast majority of these exist in the tropics, and in fact
in eastern North America there is only one species, the Ruby-throated
Hummingbird, that is responsible for flower pollination. This Hummingbird is migratory over much of its range, and the flowers it pollinates bloom
only during the months that it is present. In fact, the natural geographical
range of such plants follows closely that of the bird.

§ 211 §

Trumpet Vine flowers with
Ruby-throated Hummingbird
(Redrawn from *The Mysteries of the Flowers*
by Herbert Waldron Faulkner)

In the East, other flowers that are adapted to the Hummingbird include
Cardinal Flower, Jewelweed, Trumpet Honeysuckle, and Oswego Tea.
Trumpet Vines share many of these flowers' characteristics. It is red, long-
tubed, horizontally oriented, it produces lots of nectar, and has no scent.
The anthers of the flower are arranged against the top of the tube. The pistil
is also adjacent to the top of the flower, but projects farther than the
anthers, over the opening of the blossom. As the bird hovers in front of
the bloom and pokes its head in, any pollen that was on its head from a
previously visited flower brushes onto the pistil. Then, as the bird moves
slightly farther into the flower, its forehead touches the ripened anthers.
Dusted afresh, it will carry the new pollen to the next flower to which it
flies. It is important to remember that the bird is not "trying" to pollinate
the flowers but only trying to feed. The flower is adapted to be cross-
pollinated as a result of the bird's regular feeding habits.

The calyx at the base of the Trumpet Vine flower contains another
modification that suggests the presence of a great deal of nectar. The calyx
often evolves into a protection of the area where nectar is secreted. In
Trumpet Vine, its lobes are joined together and the whole structure much
thickened. But just as a Bumblebee can merely poke directly into the petals
of a Blueberry flower to get its nectar, a Hummingbird can do the same

§ 212 §

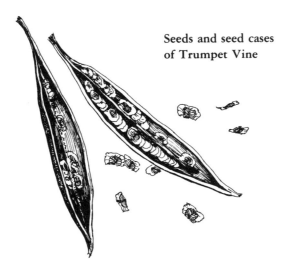

Seeds and seed cases
of Trumpet Vine

to the calyx of a Trumpet Vine. This is obviously to the disadvantage of the flower, which then does not get pollinated. I have not seen Hummingbirds gather nectar this way, but one writer has reported watching Pigeons land on Trumpet Vine and puncture the calyxes, causing an audible pop.

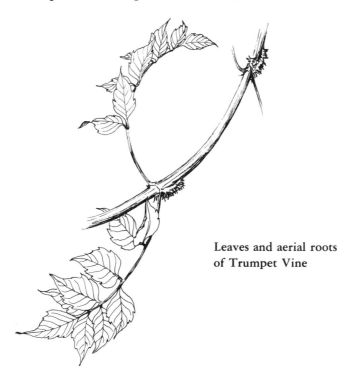

Leaves and aerial roots
of Trumpet Vine

TRUMPET VINE

The flowers later wilted and fell off. Clearly the Trumpet Vine has more evolving to do if it is going to protect itself against Pigeons.

The flowers of this species bloom from midsummer into the fall; after the first month of blooming, you will be able to watch the fruit develop. First, the united petals fall off, leaving the calyx and the pistil, which withers but remains a dried thread attached to the end of the fruit. At almost any given place on a plant, you can see a number of fruits in different stages of growth. The fruit is called a capsule, which means that it breaks open longitudinally along a number of lines, unlike the fruits of Milkweed or Spirea, which, because they break open along a single line, are considered follicles. The seeds inside the capsule are thin and bordered on either side with thin translucent wings. They fall out of the pod and drift in the wind. All plants in Trumpet Vine's family, *Bignoniaceae,* have a similar structure to their fruits and seeds. The thin, dried fruits of the Catalpa tree are another example from this family.

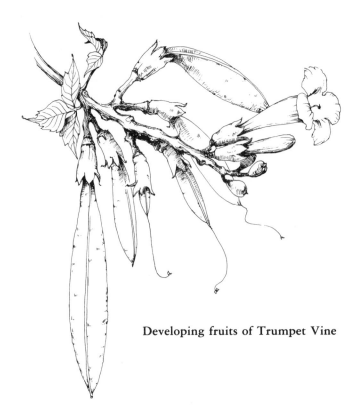

Developing fruits of Trumpet Vine

BUTTONBUSH

Cephalanthus

ORDER: *Rubiales.*   FAMILY: *Rubiaceae.*   GENUS: *Cephalanthus.*
SPECIES: *C. occidentalis,* Buttonbush.

BUTTONBUSH IS a common and widespread plant which few people take the time to know and enjoy. It grows in shallow water at the edges of ponds and rivers and is worth tracking down in any season. It has shiny green leaves throughout the warm months, beautiful blossoms in late summer, and spherical seedheads (like those of Sycamore) attached to its scraggly branches through the winter. The seedheads look a little like old-fashioned buttons and are probably the source for the plant's common name.

Maybe one of the reasons why so few people are acquainted with Buttonbush is its habitat. Unless we are avid naturalists, boaters, or fishermen, few of us explore the swampy margins of ponds and streams, where Buttonbush grows. It is often the last woody plant you encounter before getting to open water. In the shallows behind the plant you are likely to find a number of other shrubs that don't seem to like the deeper water, including Alder, Willow, Pepperbush, Azalea, and Winterberry. Because many birds like the same environment as Buttonbush, look among the plant's branches when its leaves have fallen for nests, especially those of the Song Sparrow and Red-winged Blackbird.

During the fall and winter, Buttonbush looks quite dead: its bark is peeling, its branches are scraggly, and its leaves do not emerge until late in spring. But once the leaves have fully expanded, the plant can be quite elegant, its large, glossy leaves growing in whorls of three or four. Then in late summer, when the blooming season seems to have drawn to a close, Buttonbush surprises with its white globes of blossoms and their rich, sweet fragrance filling the air. The blooms are not all that conspicuous to the eye, but they are obvious to the nose, so let your sense of smell lead you to them.

§ 215 §

BUTTONBUSH

Each of the hundreds of flowers that make up the Buttonbush inflorescence is composed of a short tubular calyx and a long tubular corolla. The flowers produce a great deal of nectar at their bases, but the long white corollas limit access to those pollinators with long mouthparts. Although butterflies and possibly some moths are the logical recipients of the blossom's nourishment, I have also seen bees and beetles crawling over the flowers and eating or collecting the pollen. If you look down inside one of the floral tubes, you will see four small yellow spots just inside. These are the anthers, which shed their pollen, even before the blossom opens, onto the immature tip of the pistil. The flower then blooms, and the pistil elongates, with the pollen at its tip. It remains in this position until an insect comes along and brushes the pollen off; the tip of the pistil then matures, becomes sticky, and with luck will receive pollen from another plant when the next insect visits. This type of pollination mechanism is often called a "brush," since the pollinator has no landing place on the flower except directly on the pistils. A similar strategy is used by the Willows.

Fall and winter are good seasons to find the spherical seedheads of Buttonbush. They range from a half inch to an inch in diameter and hang

Buttonbush in its favored habitat

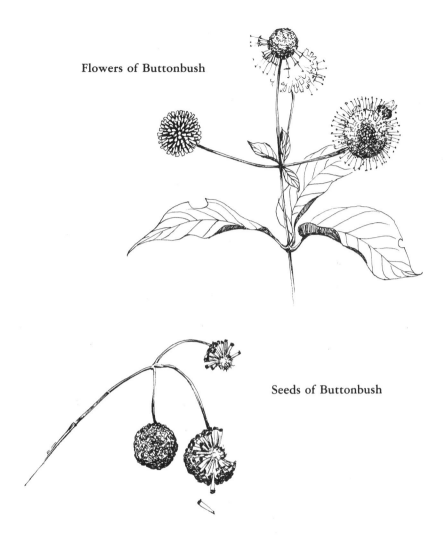

Flowers of Buttonbush

Seeds of Buttonbush

in small clusters off the tips of the branches. Packed forms in nature, such as the Buttonbush seedhead, present an interesting problem: how do you design a single unit (like one Buttonbush seed) so that when filled with hundreds of others, it will form a solid sphere? Furthermore, how does Buttonbush develop tightly packed seedheads when its flowers never get pollinated and so don't produce seeds? These problems fascinate me, and

§ 217 §

BUTTONBUSH

each time I come across some Buttonbush seedheads in winter, I like to examine them, coming a little closer to my own theory of how nature works with geometry.

As one might expect of a water plant, Buttonbush produces seeds that float, which helps disperse the plants to adjacent areas of the water. But how do the seeds get to isolated areas of water not connected by streams? Because the shrubs grow in water, their seeds are eaten primarily by ducks and provide a fairly important source of winter food. It is possible that some of the seeds get caught on the mud on the ducks' feet and then are carried to secluded ponds where the ducks like to feed.

One winter, I was snowshoeing by a small woodland pond when from quite a distance I spotted a single leaf hanging suspiciously off one of the Buttonbush plants. Since no other leaves remained on the plants, I went to investigate. I saw that the leaf had been curled around like a cigar and that inside was a large cocoon into which the leaf had been incorporated. As I looked at the branch to which the leaf was attached, I saw why it had not fallen off the bush: it was actually tied onto the twigs with webbing. Only a few cocoons are attached to twigs in winter; the largest of these are made by the Saturnids, or Silk Moths. The one I encountered was hanging, so I knew it to be the cocoon of the Promethea Moth. The cocoon of its cousin, the Cecropia Moth, is also found in winter, but it is broadly attached to a twig all along its side. The Promethea cocoons are also found on a number of other plants, such as Sassafras, Black Cherry, and Ash.

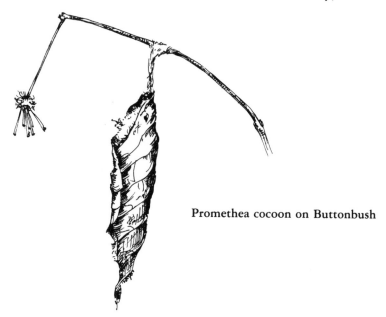

Promethea cocoon on Buttonbush

HONEYSUCKLE

Lonicera

ORDER: *Rubiales.*   FAMILY: *Caprifoliaceae.*   GENUS: *Lonicera.*
SPECIES: *L. villosa,* Mountain Fly Honeysuckle;
L. Morrowi, Morrow Honeysuckle;
L. tatarica, Tartarian Honeysuckle;
L. japonica, Japanese Honeysuckle;
L. sempervirens, Trumpet Honeysuckle, and many others.

SOMEONE ONCE POINTED OUT to me that everything on Honeysuckles is paired—their leaves, their branches, their flowers, and their fruits all appear in twos. Not only do new twigs grow in pairs, but in the following years other pairs of twigs grow from their axils. This dualism makes the branching pattern of Honeysuckles dense and brushy. I always look for characteristics of plants that will enable me to identify them in all four seasons, rather than just in the summer, and for Honeysuckles I use these multiple pairs of twigs that grow from the same spot on the branches. They are easy to see in winter and can be found in summer by merely pushing aside the leaves.

There are many species of Honeysuckles in North America, some native and some introduced. A first step in learning to distinguish them is to divide them into the shrubs and the vines. A second level of division among the shrubs can be easily made by cutting off a small twig: if it is hollow, then the shrub is introduced; if it is solid, with white pith, then the shrub is native. A similar distinction can be made among the vines: if fruits or flowers are produced all along the stems, then the plant is introduced; if the fruits or flowers are only at the tips of stems, then the vine is native.

Even though we have many native Honeysuckles, the majority of species you will encounter in the woods are introduced; of these, the most common

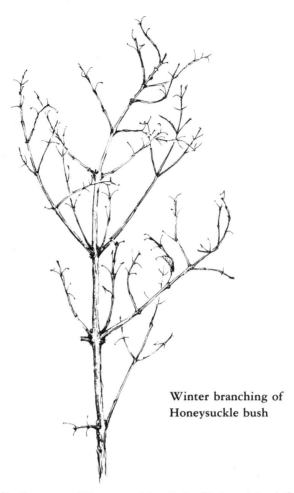

Winter branching of
Honeysuckle bush

is undoubtedly Japanese Honeysuckle. It is distinguished from all other Honeysuckle vines by having black fruits and by producing them on lateral rather than terminal branches. The plant is semi-evergreen, which means that it keeps at least a few green leaves throughout the winter. Japanese Honeysuckle is very competitive with other plants and actively climbs over vegetation. It vies with small trees for ground water, and frequently kills them by cutting out their light. The species does best in the warmer climates, since in the colder areas of the north, much of its terminal growth is killed by prolonged freezing. This factor will probably limit the range of the plant in northern areas.

HONEYSUCKLE

Tangles of Japanese Honeysuckle offer excellent cover for small mammals and nesting birds, and the fact that it keeps its leaves in winter is an added help to those birds that need roost sites or mammals that need protection from predators. The berries remain on the plant into winter and provide food for migrant and winter birds.

The extremely common introduced species of Honeysuckle shrub are Tartarian Honeysuckle and Morrow Honeysuckle. When in bloom, these species are easy to differentiate: the flowers of Tartarian are white to white-pink, while those of Morrow Honeysuckle are originally white but turn yellow after they have been pollinated. These two species produce a great many berries, which are some of the earliest fruits to be found in summer. The quick ripening makes them an important source of food for birds that are just hatching their first broods, especially Catbirds and Mockingbirds.

Over the past few years, I have looked for evidence of insects on Honeysuckle stems and leaves and have found surprisingly little. Honeysuckle is such a common plant that it seems strange that insects have not taken advantage of it. Yet the leaves are rarely eaten, and the same is true of the flowers and stems. The main insect association with the plant is in the pollination of the flowers.

All Honeysuckle flowers are pollinated in basically the same manner. The female pistil protrudes farther out of the mouth of the flower than do the male stamens. As the pollinator arrives, it first brushes against the sticky

Flowers of
Tartarian Honeysuckle

surface of the pistil, leaving pollen from a previously visited flower. Then, as the insect moves deeper into the blossom to get the nectar, it brushes against the anthers, which cover parts of its head and body with new pollen.

If you contrast the flowers of various species of Honeysuckle, you will notice that the tube formed by their joined petals is of varying lengths. The longer the tube, the more difficult it is for certain flower-visitors to reach the nectar. In some species, such as Mountain Fly Honeysuckle, the corolla tubes are fairly short, which indicates that a variety of insects can reach the nectar. But in species like Japanese Honeysuckle, the tube is too long and narrow for most insects. Only butterflies and moths, which have long, thin mouthparts that they can uncoil and project down the floral tube, can obtain the nectar. But Japanese Honeysuckle has specialized its pollination mechanism to an even greater extent. Its new blooms open at dusk, when they give off their sweetest fragrance. These traits are both adaptations to Sphinx moths, species that search for food in the early evening and hover before the flowers while they sip the nectar. They look like giant Bumblebees or Hummingbirds as they dart about in the dusk, seeking out untapped blooms.

The Trumpet Honeysuckle is the only species with a floral tube longer than that of the Japanese Honeysuckle. Its tube is too long even for the

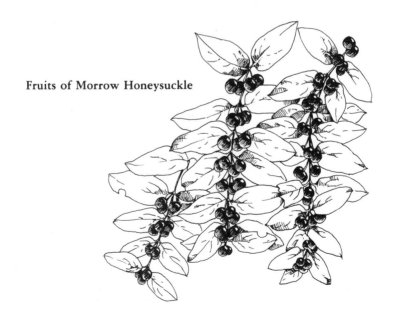

Fruits of Morrow Honeysuckle

Trumpet Honeysuckle

Sphinx's mouthparts; in addition, the flower has no odor to attract the insects, and its red color makes it difficult to locate in the dark. All these characteristics point to a flower that is adapted to Hummingbirds. In the East, our only species is the Ruby-throated Hummingbird. Hummingbird flowers are described in greater detail in the Trumpet Vine section. Honeysuckles are a marvelous example of how different species in the same genus show varying degrees of pollinator specialization.

I remember how as a young boy I used to run with my brothers and sister to an old field a few houses away, where lots of Honeysuckle grew. A special activity at this spot was picking off the blooms and sucking the "honey" from the back of the flowers. Even now when I come across Honeysuckle I do this, and always take a moment to compare the present taste with the sweetness of the last flower I tried. I find that moments like these add a great deal to my enjoyment of plants. We need these types of relationships to our natural environment—strong experiential associations. They should not stop with our youth but continue throughout our lives. The Honeysuckle flowers are always there for us to discover, whether it be through taste, smell, sight, or simply through taking pleasure in their function.

VIBURNUM

Viburnum

ORDER: *Rubiales.*   FAMILY: *Caprifoliaceae.*   GENUS: *Viburnum.*
SPECIES: *V. alnifolium,* Hobblebush; *V. cassinoides,* Witherod;
V. nudum, Possum Haw; *V. Lentago,* Sweet Viburnum;
V. prunifolium, Black Haw; *V. dentatum,* Arrow-wood;
V. acerifolium, Maple-leaved Viburnum; *V. edule,* Squashberry;
V. trilobum, Highbush Cranberry, and others.

THE VIBURNUMS ARE the classical shrubs of the woods. They are stately
plants, each species a prominent member of its preferred habitat; their
leaves are finely cut, their flowers blossom in generous umbels, and their
fruits are rich, dark colors. No other genus among our shrubs has as many
distinct individuals—so distinct that to the beginner they may seem like
unrelated plants. Even the common names that they have acquired over the
centuries—Arrow-wood, Hobblebush, Nannyberry, Witherod, Wild Raisin, Possum Haw, Highbush Cranberry, and Stagbush—suggest their
unique personalities.

But obviously, Viburnums would not be in the same genus if they didn't
share some important characteristics. One of these features is that they all
have opposite leaves. While this feature is present in many genera of
shrubs, plants with opposite leaves remain in the minority. Another trait
common to the Viburnums is the structure of their flowers and the shape
of their flower clusters. The blossoms are arranged in umbrella-shaped
clusters; each bloom is composed of five sepals, five petals, five stamens, and
one to three pistils. Those aspects of Viburnums that vary greatly among
species are manner of growth, leaf shapes, and the appearance of winter
buds.

For the purposes of recognition, the Viburnums are often divided into
four groups, based on the four major leaf shapes of our native species. One

VIBURNUM

group, which has leaves that look roughly like those of Maples, includes Maple-leaved Viburnum and Highbush Cranberry. Highbush Cranberry is one of the most confusing common names for a shrub; the plant is not at all related to the Cranberries, plants that are actually in an entirely different family. Its name refers to its bright-red fruits. When cooked with some lemon and sugar, they can pass as a substitute for Cranberries. The plant is generally a tall, arching shrub with numerous stems, growing in or near the edge of woods. Its shiny red translucent fruits make the shrub easy to identify in fall and winter; the berries are a beautiful sight, contrasting sharply with the snow or muted colors of the woods. Even though I know that the fruits taste ghastly when eaten raw, it is hard for me to resist trying one each winter; they look so inviting on the plant, and somewhere in the back of my mind I believe that I will come across a sweet one.

In the understory of older woods is another Viburnum with a maple leaf shape, aptly named Maple-leaved Viburnum. This is a beautiful but modest

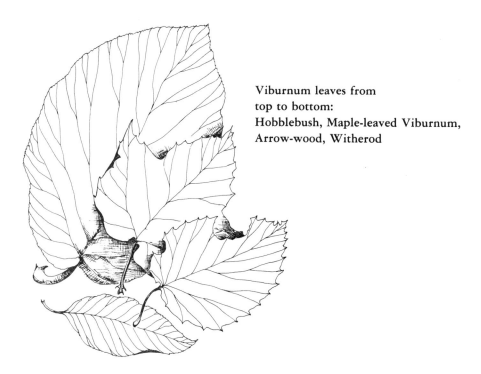

Viburnum leaves from
top to bottom:
Hobblebush, Maple-leaved Viburnum,
Arrow-wood, Witherod

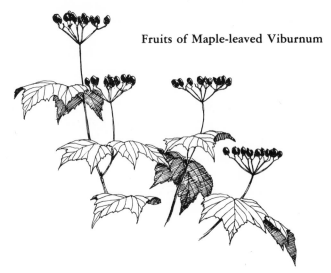

Fruits of Maple-leaved Viburnum

plant, usually found in small groups that have been created by vegetative growth from rootstocks. It is a very graceful shrub, often only four to five feet high, and it holds its maturing fruits up into the air like a fine candelabrum. If you look only at its leaves, it is very hard to tell Maple-leaved Viburnum from Highbush Cranberry, but when the plants are in bloom, they are easy to distinguish. Both have flat clusters of creamy white flowers, but surrounding those of Highbush Cranberry is a row of blooms with much larger petals. If you look closely at these blossoms, you will see that they have neither pistils nor stamens. They are in fact sterile, probably evolved to help advertise the presence of the smaller, fertile flowers in the center of the cluster. Only one other native Viburnum, Hobblebush, has this type of floral arrangement, though it is also seen in the Hydrangeas.

Highbush Cranberry showing sterile and fertile flowers

VIBURNUM

Hobblebush is easily distinguished from Highbush Cranberry by its large heart-shaped leaves and its habit of trailing along the ground as it grows. I find this manner of growth the plant's most interesting trait. The stems arch over, send down roots where they touch the ground, and then arch up and over again. This configuration explains the plant's common name: when a domestic animal is hobbled, a length of rope is connected to two of its legs to limit the length of its step. Hobblebush is definitely a woodland plant. It prefers moist soils and is often found in rocky mountainous areas. (In many portions of the White Mountains in New England, it is the only understory shrub.) Its manner of growth may be particularly well suited to a rocky glacial area. In such an environment, whatever soil is available exists in isolated crevasses of rocks. Hobblebush's habit of rooting at the tips of its branches would then help it take advantage of these bits of soil and spread leaves out over the barren areas in between. The berries of the plant turn bright red in late summer and fall, and then dark purple or black for the remainder of their time on the plant. Another time when Hobblebush distinguishes itself is in midwinter, when its leaf buds are large and have no protective scales, so that you can easily see the two

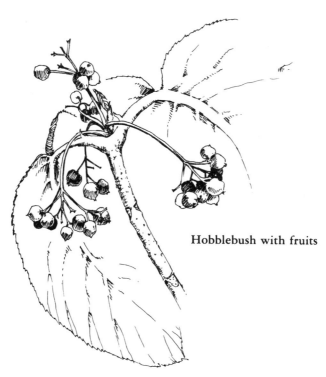

Hobblebush with fruits

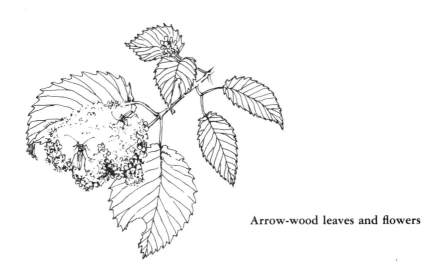

Arrow-wood leaves and flowers

unopened leaves folded neatly together. The flower buds, when present, are round, about a half inch in diameter, and placed between two leaves.

Since Hobblebush is the only one of our native Viburnum species with a large heart-shaped leaf, it forms a group in itself. A third type of Viburnum leaf is shared by at least four common species. This leaf shape is roughly oval, and pointed at the tip; it has all around its margins sharp serrations that look a little like the teeth of a wood saw. This group is often called the Arrowwoods. The member species typically have many long stems growing from the same spot. I have found some that had arched over to the ground and even rooted at their tips like Hobblebush, but this is not common. Whether or not this plant was really used for making arrows, it certainly could have been. The stems are extremely hard and tough, they grow straight with an even diameter, and in some cases they are actually angled with six partially flattened surfaces. The various species of the Arrowwoods are distinguished by the relative hairiness of their twigs and the size of the serrations on their leaves.

The last set of Viburnums is characterized by its fairly narrow, lance-shaped leaves whose margins are either smooth or finely toothed. This group includes the species with the sweetest wild fruits. Those of Black Haw and Southern Black Haw are the best, and when well ripened, they can be enjoyed right off the plant; the fruits of Witherod, sometimes known as Wild Raisin, are also good eating. Each of these fruits varies in the

§ 228 §

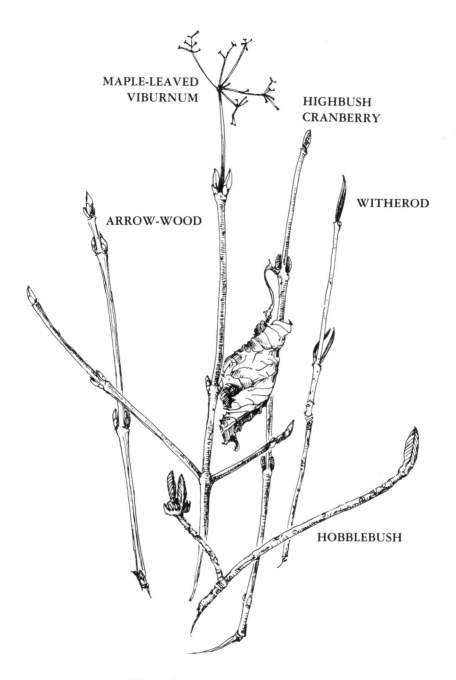

MAPLE-LEAVED
VIBURNUM

HIGHBUSH
CRANBERRY

ARROW-WOOD

WITHEROD

HOBBLEBUSH

Winter buds of common Viburnums

amount of pulp surrounding its seed. I have found that the taste varies widely even within species, so I always nibble the fruits cautiously at first.

Viburnums in this group have long, thin leaf buds that are enclosed in a pair of leaf scales. The leaf scales have a granular appearance and are either gray or red-brown. I love to watch these buds open in spring, and consider the event the most beautiful moment of the year for these species. First, the long rough scales are shed and pairs of leaves open in perfect unison. Their sides are folded up along the midvein, their exterior is reddish and granular like the bud scales, and their finely cut teeth look like jewels along the edge of the leaf when seen with the light behind them. Framed by the graceful lines of the opposite twigs, these features create a curving symmetry. Visit these plants in this season and see if you don't agree.

When I was learning to identify shrubs and vines, I started by becoming acquainted with all the most frequently encountered species—the Brambles, the Dogwoods, the Blueberries, and a few others. I then began to pay attention to the next most common species; it was here that I discovered all the Viburnums. Except for Hobblebush, these plants never cover large areas of woods or fields like the Sumacs or Dogwoods; rather, they are found as small groups scattered about the forests, thriving in their own special niches.

ELDERBERRY

Sambucus

ORDER: *Rubiales.* FAMILY: *Caprifoliaceae.* GENUS: *Sambucus.*
SPECIES: *S. canadensis,* Common Elderberry;
S. pubens, Red Elderberry.

IN WINTER, Elderberry is a ragged mass of warty branchings, stems of all
ages, both living and dead, clustered together in the same area. Even the
living stems are extremely brittle, breaking off in your hand like dry twigs
and giving off a faint odor some describe as unpleasant. Because in this
season the stems can be easily hollowed out and made into tubes, they were
used by the Indians and early settlers as spiles for tapping the sap from
Maple trees.

It always seems a bit of a miracle when, in late spring, leaves start to grow
on the stalks that looked so lifeless in winter. These leaves are long and
pinnately compound, and they quickly clothe the plants in a lush dark
green. The large umbels of flowers emerge soon afterward. Before they
open, examine each cluster, for you are likely to find some of the flower
buds swollen to twice the size of the others. These buds have had eggs laid
in them by the Elder Flower Midge, *Youngomyia umbellicola,* and are now
in the process of transforming into galls. The midge larva matures inside
the bud, preventing its blooming.

There are two main species of Elderberry in eastern North America.
They differ in the color of their pith, the arrangement of their flowers, and
the color of their fruits. Common Elderberry, the most widespread, has
white pith, a flat umbel of flowers, and dark-purple-to-black fruits. It grows
best in open areas with moist, rich soil. Red Elderberry's pith is brown, its
flowers are arranged in a panicle, and its fruits are bright red. Although it
has much the same range as Common Elderberry, Red Elderberry is more
often found in rocky upland areas and within woods.

§ 231 §

Elderberry in summer

One summer, at about the time when the Elderberry flowers were in bloom, I went out to look for insects on the plants and came across one of the most spectacular beetles that I had ever seen. It was about an inch long, with wing covers that were pumpkin orange at their base and iridescent steel blue at their tips. It also had long jointed antennae that looked like horns. There were a number of these beetles on the flowerheads of the plants, so I captured one live in a jar and took it home for identification. It turned out that the beetle was right where it should have been, on Elderberry, for it was an Elder Borer, *Desmocerus palliatus.* The borer lays its eggs on the stems in summer, and the larvae bore within the stems, where they remain until they are mature. These insects are not commonly seen, but if you remember to look on Elderberry plants when the flowers have just started to bloom, you have a good chance of spotting one. After learning about my captured beetle, I released it back on the plants.

The fruits of Elderberries ripen in mid to late summer and are often so numerous that they weigh the branches down. They are eaten by many species of birds and of course have always been used by humans as well.

§ 232 §

Elder borer
on Elderberry twigs

Elderberries ripening
in late summer

ELDERBERRY

The fruits are tiny drupes, which limits their food uses for us; the large seeds are too hard to chew and must be strained out before jams or jellies can be made. Still, I never pass an Elderberry plant with ripe fruits without taking a few in my hand to eat, just to see if I have chanced upon an individual plant producing particularly tasty berries.

I once read that solitary wasps used old Elderberry stems as brood chambers. This phenomenon fascinated me and I decided to go out and see it for myself. I collected about a dozen dead stems that seemed likely candidates and shared opening them up with friends. After we had opened the first six, we had quite a list of contents, including spider cocoons, earwigs, mud, ants, and strangely enough, a sunflower seed—but no solitary wasps. Then in the last half dozen we were lucky enough to find two

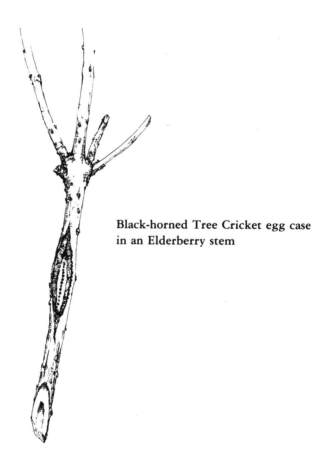

Black-horned Tree Cricket egg case
in an Elderberry stem

ELDERBERRY

examples of what we were looking for. The soft pith of the stems had been hollowed out and a series of chambers had been created inside. The chambers were about an inch long and were divided by sections of an unidentified material that was tightly packed. In each chamber was a small white wasp larva and some stored food. At the proper time the larvae would pupate and emerge from the hollowed stem as adults. I have since gone to Elderberries in summer to watch the wasps at work, with the result that I now consider them among my favorite insects. It is extremely entertaining to watch them drop bits of sawdust out of the ends of the stems and then make numerous trips to cache their larval chambers with food. Other shrub stems with soft pith, such as those of Blackberry and Sumac, are also used by the wasps.

There is another fascinating insect signature left on the stems of Elderberry, one that has the appearance of a zipper installed in the bark of the plant. The bark is split longitudinally for about three inches; all along either side of the split are little indentations. This construction is the former egg-laying area of the Black-horned Tree Cricket, a relative of the famous songster the Snowy Tree Cricket or Temperature Cricket. In summer, the cricket crawls up onto the new stems of an Elderberry, makes a series of small holes in the bark with her ovipositor, and lays an egg in each hole. The eggs overwinter in the stem and the young crickets emerge in the spring. As the plant continues to grow, the bark splits along the row of holes. These egg-laying sites can be found on the twigs of Swamp Dogwood as well.

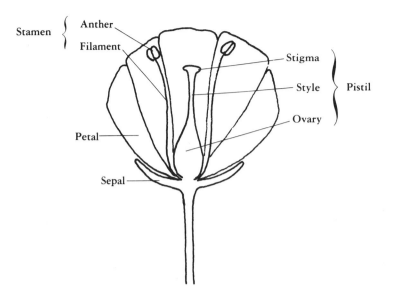

Stamen { Anther

Filament

Stigma

Style } Pistil

Ovary

Petal

Sepal

PARTS OF A FLOWER

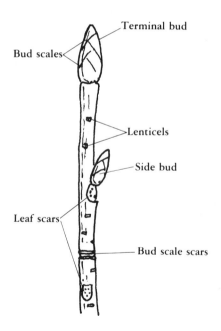

Terminal bud

Bud scales

Lenticels

Side bud

Leaf scars

Bud scale scars

PARTS OF A TWIG

GLOSSARY

ACHENE. A hard, dry fruit consisting of a single seed contained in a covering that does not split open.

AERIAL ROOT. A rootlike growth produced above ground.

ANGIOSPERM. A large group of plants characterized mainly by the maturation of seeds inside the carpel or female part of the plant.

ANTHER. The part of a flower that produces pollen.

ARIL. A structure covering a seed and originating from the point at which the seed is attached to the stem rather than from floral parts. It is technically not part of the fruit.

AXIL. The upper angle between a leaf and stem.

CALYX. The row of sepals on the outer edge of a flower.

COMPOUND LEAF. A leaf that is composed of smaller leaflets.

CAPSULE. A dry fruit that, when mature, splits open into more than one section.

COROLLA. The row of petals in a flower.

CARPEL. The female part of a flower, containing ovary and ovules.

DIOECIOUS. Refers to species that produce male and female flowers on separate plants.

DRUPE. A fleshy fruit with a hard stone or pit that contains one seed.

FOLLICLE. A dry fruit that, when mature, splits down one side.

FRUIT. The seed-bearing part of a plant, including the seed and its covering.

GALL. A deformation of plant tissue caused by an insect's secretions or mechanical actions.

LANCEOLATE. Shaped like the point of a spear or lance.

LENTICEL. A small opening in the bark that allows gaseous exchange with the atmosphere.

MINE. A trail that marks where an insect has eaten between the layers of a leaf.

OPPOSITE LEAVES. A pair of leaves that grow directly across from each other on a stem.

OVULE. The egg, or that part of the plant which develops into the seed after being fertilized.

GLOSSARY

PALMATE LEAF. A compound leaf in which the leaflets are joined at a single point and radiate outward like the fingers from the palm of a hand.

PANICLE. An arrangement of flower clusters branching from a central stem.

PEDICEL. The final stem that supports a flower.

PETAL. The component part of a corolla.

PETIOLE. The stalk of a leaf.

PINNATE LEAF. A compound leaf in which leaflets are arranged on either side of a central axis.

PISTIL. The female part of a flower.

PITH. The central, interior portion of a stem.

POLYGAMOUS. Having both unisexual and bisexual flowers on the same plant.

PROTANDROUS. Bisexual flowers in which the male parts mature before the female parts.

PROTOGYNOUS. Bisexual flowers in which the female parts mature before the male parts.

RACEME. An arrangement of single flowers along a main axis.

RECEPTACLE. The base of a flower from which all of the flower parts grow.

RHIZOME. An underground stem that periodically sends down roots and sends up shoots.

ROOTSTOCK. A rhizome.

SAMARA. A small fruit with an attached wing that aids it in being carried by the wind.

SEPAL. An individual part of the calyx.

SIMPLE LEAF. A single leaf with no leaflet subdivisions.

SINUATE. Wavy, or shaped like an "s."

STAMEN. The male part of the flower.

STIGMA. The tip of the pistil, where pollen adheres.

STOLON. A horizontal stem that grows above the ground and roots at various points.

INDEX

Italic numbers refer to illustrations

INDEX

INDEX

INDEX

INDEX

§ 243 §

INDEX